What's Next for the Economy

Using the Power of Cycles to Predict "What's Next" for Inflation, the Stock Market, Real Estate, and Business

Edward Thomas

ACCE Publishing LLC

ACCE Publishing LLC
1 League, Unit 62422
Irvine, California 92602

What's Next for the Economy / Edward Thomas. —1st ed.
Library of Congress Control Number: 2017903045
ISBN 978-0-9983281-0-2 (Hardbound)
ISBN 978-0-9983281-1-9 (Paperback)
ISBN 978-0-9983281-2-6 (eBook)

Contents

for AT, CAT, CKT, GMT, and JET

Life and commerce are like the seasons.

—JIM ROHN

Prologue

Timing **is** everything. In order to succeed in life, it doesn't just matter **what** you do. It matters just as much **when** you do it. Throughout this book, I will relate personal experiences and my rationale to explain why I believe **what** will happen and **when** it will occur. I hope these personal notes will be somewhat of a cautionary tale for those of you who have not experienced these events, and that they provide a bit of assurance or sympathy for those of you who have.

I feel like somewhat of an "everyman" – or an average guy who has experienced over the past 40 years what most people have experienced: the inflation of the late 1970s and early 1980s, the stock market crash of 1987 and the real estate boom of the late 1980s, the Greenspan era of economic prosperity in the 1990s and the stock market crash of 2000, the real estate frenzy of 2001–2006, and the economic crisis of 2008. From these experiences, I have drawn a set of observations, which I have put forth in this book.

This is not a book for the "experts." Economists, bankers, Wall Street brokers, and the people you see on CNN or MSNBC or Bloomberg, they know all this information already. That is why they are on these shows and providing the services they provide. What I feel is missing is the big picture of how it all plays together – the relationships and interrelationships between inflation and real estate, real estate and the stock market, and the business cycle and everything else. I wrote this book for the general public – for people like me, who have mistimed the market and missed opportunities along the way.

In order to better communicate the concepts discussed in this book, I thought it would be a good idea to describe what I mean by a "cycle." For those of you already familiar with this subject, you may want to skip this paragraph: A cycle describes a full rotation or circuit of a wave, from the starting point to the end point, before it repeats itself. Cycles are typically thought of as a sinusoidal trace, from the initial or zero position, up to the maximum positive value, then back down the positive area through zero to the most negative position, and back up through the negative area up to zero. See Figure 1 for the graphical illustration of a typical sinusoidal cycle. Cycles can have different shapes and amplitudes (distance from the mean or zero value), and the one below is represented here purely for illustrative purposes.

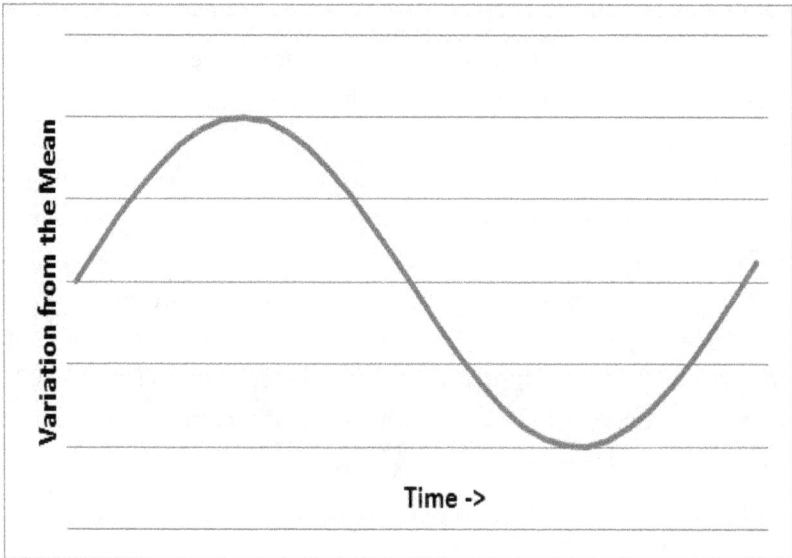

Figure 1. A Typical Sinusoidal Cycle

This book is designed to describe four different cycles (inflation, the stock market, real estate, and business) in the same format and context by:

1. describing the "up" portion of the cycle,
2. describing the "down" portion of the cycle,
3. describing the overall cycle length and providing historical evidence to verify the period of the cycle, and

4. based on the preceding information, providing specific data explaining what will occur next in the cycle (incorporating where we currently are on each cycle).

What's Next for the Economy is a book about economic cycles and how they can be used to project current economic conditions forward to understand what to expect in the future. If you can learn from history, you can take advantage of that knowledge for your own personal planning and decision making. The key question in projecting the past to determine the future (or at least getting an idea of where it's headed) is to know where the economy is in each particular cycle. You need to know at what point of the curve it's on, so you can tell what the next point will be, to answer the question, "What's next?" The value of this approach to understanding the economy is that it is not time-specific: If you know where you are in each cycle, you can project to where you will be in that cycle for future dates at any time. This makes investment planning a much easier task for everyone interested in his or her own financial future.

Inflation

I nflation will be the biggest worldwide economic challenge in the next 20 years. Though I was young at the time, I experienced firsthand the effects of inflation during the up phase of the last major inflationary cycle. Current events are eerily similar. Think of the 1960s–1970s: The United States was fighting a war in Vietnam, President Johnson had declared a War on Poverty, and we had just endured the first of many oil shocks to come – the 1973 OPEC/Arab Oil Embargo. This last inflationary cycle, which was exacerbated by economic policy, didn't end until 1982.

Consider how that period of US history compares to current events and economic conditions: We have been at war with terrorists in Iraq and Afghanistan since 2001. President Obama pushed through Congress the Affordable Care Act, or ACA, and due to the extenuating circumstances of the Great Recession of 2007–2009, created the largest budget deficit in US history. All we need now to complete the analogy is an oil shock, which I believe is just around the corner, as I will explain in the next chapters.

At this time, inflation is so benign that people don't even think about it. In fact, some people are more worried about deflation than inflation. However, all this will change in the coming years, and we all need to prepare and plan for the eventual and inevitable pendulum swing to the other side of the inflation cycle.

Chapter 1.
The Great Inflation

The Great Inflation started with the economic policies of the Kennedy and Johnson administrations in the 1960s, and it ended during the first term of President Reagan's administration in 1982. The Great Inflation was certainly compounded by other economic and political events of that era, including the OPEC oil embargo, US grain sales to Russia, the Cold War, the Vietnam War, President Johnson's "War on Poverty," and the civil rights movement. Low levels of inflation, in general, promote price stability and a healthy economy. However, high levels of persistent inflation, such as those experienced during the Great Inflation, cause uncertainty and doubt – inflation takes away people's faith in the future, because they don't know what prices to expect or what price shock will happen next.

Robert J. Samuelson, in a book titled *The Great Inflation and Its Aftermath*, provides a key concept: The reason for the Great Inflation was an idea. That idea was the concept of "full employment." "In the 1960s, academic economists argued – and political leaders accepted – that the economy could be kept permanently near "full employment" (initially defined as 4 percent unemployment)."[1] The concept of full employment was simple – by using the unemployment rate as your guide, you can manage the economy to attain the maximum possible level of employment in the country. Politicians like to say they are bringing jobs to their respective districts, because that is what keeps voters happy and gets the politicians re-elected. However, by focusing too much on the ideal – in addition to a misunderstanding of the real level of unemployment that is equivalent to full employment – the government actually made inflation worse.

The policy makers in the White House, in conjunction with the economic advisors and staff at the Federal Reserve, were targeting a full employment level that translated to a 3% to 4% unemployment rate.[2] That is much lower than the now academically accepted meaning of "full employment," which is 5-6% unemployment (there is always a minimum level of joblessness – frictional unemployment – that is due to staff turnover, seasonal staffing, summer jobs for students, etc., that cannot be eliminated). This became known as the non-accelerating inflation rate of unemployment (NAIRU). Any unemployment level of less than NAIRU causes wage inflation, due to competition for scarce labor resources. This means that economic policy and policy decisions, if not directly the causes of the persistent and intransigent inflation of the 1970s, certainly made it worse.

It is also interesting to note that the Federal Reserve's stated goals for Federal Open Market Committee (FOMC) activity are an inflation rate of about 2% and unemployment rates of 5.2% to 6% (the "dual mandate" of low inflation and low unemployment discussed in former Fed Chairman Ben Bernanke's speech at a conference for the National Bureau of Economic Research, Cambridge, Massachusetts, on July 10, 2013).[3] This means that the Fed's monetary policy objectives are similar to those carried out by his predecessors in the 1970s.

THE MONEY SUPPLY AND INFLATION

Inflation typically occurs when too many dollars in the money supply are chasing too few goods. The money supply, as of the writing of this book, is at an all-time high. In an attempt to pull the economy out of the worst recession since the Great Depression, the US Treasury has pumped one trillion dollars into the money supply. However, it seems this money has not flowed into the economy, as most analysts (especially economists and the president's advisors) would have expected. At least, that is the perception.

I learned about the money supply and the velocity of money in my macroeconomics class in college. The concept is well explained in *The Age of Uncertainty* by John Kenneth Galbraith. Money supply became a major topic of discussion in the inflationary age of the 1970s. In his book, which became a television series on PBS, the Public Broadcasting Service, Galbraith explains Irving Fisher's equation and its consequences: Prices are determined by the amount of money in circulation times its velocity – the number of times it changes hands – divided by the number of transactions.

The following chart of US annual inflation figures from 1948 to 2011 shows the rise and fall of inflation over the last 60 years, which approximately mirror the last Kondratieff cycle (I will further explain and define the Kondratieff cycle later in this section). This figure also shows a fourth-order curve fit of the data, depicting the natural cycle of inflation data, which reveals a Kondratieff wave. Figure 2 provides a clue as to where inflation rates should be headed – higher.

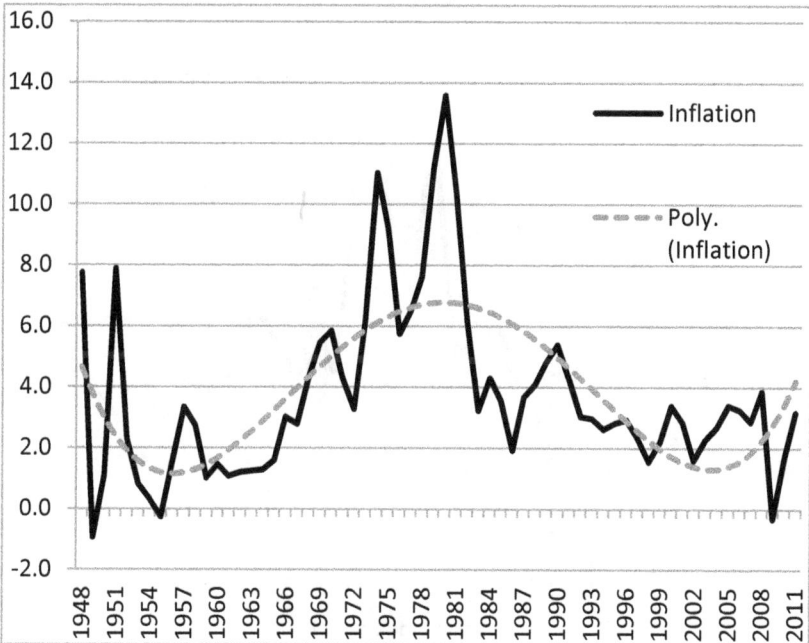

Figure 2. Annual US Inflation (1948-2011)[4]

THE PHILLIPS CURVE

In 1958, an economist from New Zealand named William Phillips wrote a paper describing the relationship between unemployment and the rate of change in wages over time. In this paper, "The Relation between Unemployment and the Rate of Change of Money Wage Rates in the United Kingdom, 1861-1957," Phillips described an inverse relationship between inflation and unemployment. This is now known as the "Phillips Curve." The implication here was that, by economic policy design or executive decision, the economy could expand with more jobs (less unemployment) at the expense of a little inflation. This becomes important in our discussion on the causes of the Great Inflation, because it induced economists of the 1960s to strongly believe in their ability to control and manage the economy. Figure 3 graphically shows over a 60-year period the relationship between unemployment and inflation.

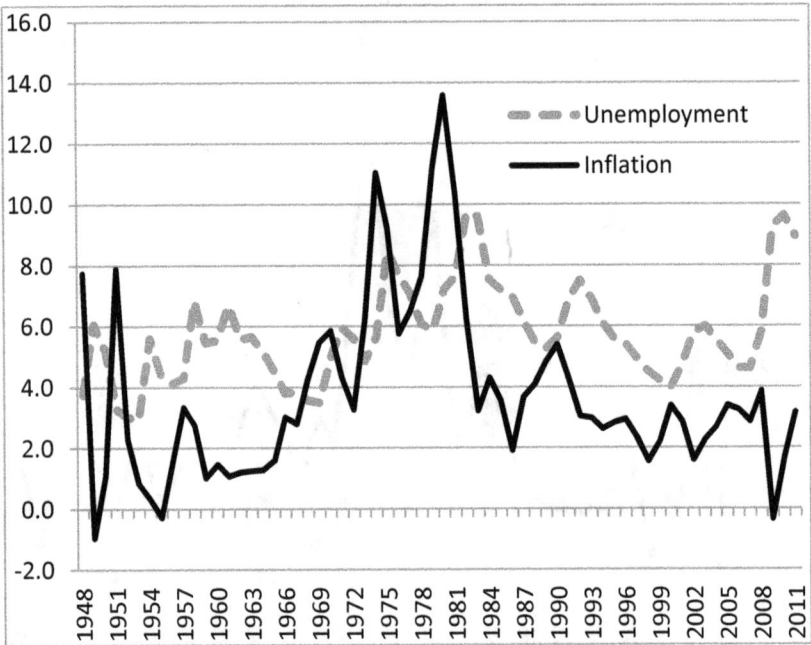

Figure 3. Inflation versus Unemployment (1948-2011)[5]

Figure 2 shows only the inflation rate over time. Figure 3 shows the relationship of unemployment to inflation over that same time period. This graphically describes a near-inverse relationship between unemployment and inflation. The good news is that, as inflation goes up, unemployment should fall.

PRESIDENT JOHNSON'S 'GREAT SOCIETY'

By the middle of President Johnson's term, the country was in the midst of the Vietnam War and continuing the Cold War against the Soviets. The president had also begun several new government spending programs. The "Great Society" programs he created included the Social Security Act of 1965, which spawned Medicare and Medicaid, and the 1965 Elementary and Secondary Education Act, which provides federal funds for education at the local level. He called these programs a "war on poverty."

The Great Society programs called for billions of dollars of new funding for programs like the Jobs Corps, the Volunteers in Service to America (VISTA), the Neighborhood Youth Corps, the Model Cities Program, Upward Bound, and the Food Stamp Act of 1964. In addition, $1.1 billion was sent to the states to fund education under the Elementary and Secondary Education Act.[6] Medicaid funding was also provided to states to fund medical coverage for welfare recipients. Finally, the Medicare program was expanded to include anyone over 65 years of age, regardless of need. These are only some of the programs that were created and/or funded as a result of President Johnson's efforts.

As a corollary to President Johnson's Great Society programs, President Obama was spending vast amounts of government funding on programs for health care, housing, and debt relief. Obamacare is a $1.3 trillion government program, and during the housing crisis, an estimated $1 trillion was pumped into the US economy.[7] As of December 31, 2016, the federal debt was $20.0 trillion and rising.[8] The administration is also dealing with the costs of twin antiterrorist wars in Iraq and Afghanistan. All that is needed now is an oil shock to complete the similarities to the Great Inflation conditions of the 1970s.

I wasn't driving yet at the time, but if you are of a certain age, you will remember the long gasoline queues during the 1973 OPEC oil embargo. Cars were lined up around the block at every gas station to pump those few precious drops. Vehicles with even-numbered plates were allowed to pump gas on certain days and those with odd-numbered plates on the other days. People started taking on a hoarder's mentality – they would drive around on a three-quarter-full tank looking for somewhere to top it off. In addition, people would get into fights if someone tried to cut into the long lines at gas stations.[9] I also remember my mother complaining about the high costs of bread and meat.

PRICE CONTROLS AND INFLATION

All through the 1970s and early 1980s, inflation was persistent and endemic. President Johnson had famously used his own considerable personality and charisma to strong-arm unions and corporations to keep wages and prices under control.[10] President Nixon employed price controls during his administration, as did Presidents Ford and Carter. If you are my age, you might remember the WIN button – "Whip Inflation Now" was President Gerald Ford's slogan. He attempted to get public support for price controls and tried to focus on the inflation issue, but he was derailed during his presidency by the backlash from his pardon of President Nixon.[11]

Price controls are typically established during times of war, when certain materials and commodities are rationed to meet combat needs. This rationing leads to price increases (inflation), due to the limited amount of supply available. Thus, price controls are usually enforced to minimize the impact of this temporary condition. But this was not the case for the price controls established by Johnson, Nixon, Ford, and Carter. Their price control policies were usually temporary measures that ended up being permanent, because once they were put into effect, the general public enjoyed the predictability of steady prices. The group that was most aggravated by price-wage controls was organized labor. Labor unions threatened "war" over it.[12]

President Nixon took the historic step of closing the gold window in 1971, at the same time that he announced new wage and price controls for the country. In addition, he announced a tax cut for individuals and businesses and a 10% tax increase on imports. These measures were called the New Economic Policy (NEP). The NEP was actually intended to ensure Nixon's re-election in 1972.[13] Nixon won re-election in a land-slide, partly due to the good economic conditions that had developed by the summer of 1972. To that end, the NEP proved successful. However, it did nothing to reduce or rein in inflation.

President Carter did not fare any better than his predecessors when it came to the battle with inflation. He also tried price controls, and he worked with unions and labor leaders in an attempt to curtail wage in-creases.[14] However, his formula for dealing with inflation didn't work, and I believe that it proved to be his undoing – in addition to the Iran hostage crisis. During the last year of his term, Iranian students overran the American Embassy in Tehran, and personnel in the embassy were taken hostage. This, in addition to inflation and economic conditions, was what caused President Carter to lose the 1980 presidential election to former California governor Ronald Reagan. President Reagan took office in January 1981, when Paul Volcker was Fed chair.

INFLATION EXPECTATIONS

It was my first year out of school. I had graduated from the University of Michigan with a bachelor's degree in aerospace engineering, and I had gone to work for TRW in Redondo Beach, California, in June of 1980. I had been working for approximately eight months when I received my first performance evaluation and merit review. This was an annual event, when engineers were evaluated against their peers and given a raise, based on their contributions to the corporation.

As this was my first experience working for a major corporation and my first performance evaluation, I didn't know what to expect for a raise. What I received was 17%. Since this was the first year of what was to become a 30-year career in the aerospace industry, I had no idea that I would never again receive that much of a raise. I found out later that some of my peers received 20% raises. As it turned out, inflation was running at about 13% in the prior year, so my effective raise was only 4%.

So, the expectation of inflation is as bad as the effective level of inflation, in that it is a never-ending cycle of ever-increasing prices that raise the demand for wage hikes, which cause producers to jack up prices to offset the wage increases and to maintain profit levels. This is called the wage-price spiral, and it is what drives hyperinflation, which the United States has only experienced a few times in its history. There was hyperinflation during the American War of Independence – it reached as high as 40% during those years. Inflation hit 20% during the Civil War, but it was much higher in the South, due to the Northern blockade of Southern ports, which choked their supply of goods and imported products while limiting the sale of Southern crops. Inflation broke over 24% during World War I (see Figure 4).[15]

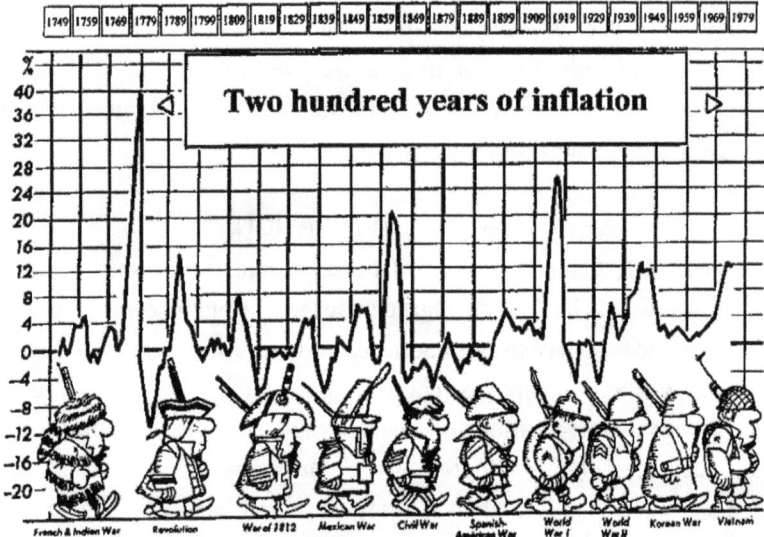

Figure 4. Inflation and War (courtesy of A. Gary Shilling & Co, Inc)

PAUL VOLCKER TO THE RESCUE

It wasn't until Paul Volcker came along that anyone found an effective tool to stop inflation. He was the Fed chair from 1979 to 1987 – he held on for two four-year terms – and he radically and forcefully put an end to the expectation of higher prices by squeezing the life out of the economy. He increased the federal funds rate and constricted the money supply, reducing the number of bills in circulation. This caused one of the worst recessions on record. The 1981–1982 recession was extremely severe and caused significant reductions in GDP and employment. Unemployment ran at over 10% in November and December of 1982.[16]

Economists debated whether the federal funds rate or the money supply (M1, or the total amount of cash and money in checking accounts readily available for purchasing goods) was the best lever to affect or reduce inflation. The monetarists, led by Milton Friedman, believed reducing the total volume of money in the system would reduce inflation. The Keynesian economists believed in managing aggregate demand through fiscal policy (taxes, expenditures, and interest rates) to control prices. Paul Volcker proved that it is the money supply that best tames the inflation beast.

Money supply will probably be the tool used in future dealings with inflation; however, will it be as effective next time, if everyone is expecting the Fed to use it? I think the answer to that question is probably yes, as there will be a physical limit to the number of dollars in the system available to purchase goods and services. The question is, will there be a Paul Volcker-type around the next time to do the dirty work of squeezing the excess out of the economy, at the expense of his or her own political career?

By using these tools and forcing the economy to go through a serious recession, Volcker ended the Great Inflation. The good news was, it worked. The bad news was, it was one of the worst recessions in recent memory. This is probably why he didn't serve a third term as Fed chair. Critics were calling for his head on a platter long before the fruits of his labor showed. He was called before Congress many times to explain his policies and defend his plan for defeating inflation – legislators were impatient that it was taking so long for his plan to work. Even within President Reagan's administration, Volcker's efforts were not completely appreciated. In *American Banker*, Martin Mayer wrote an article about Paul Volcker and President Reagan's relationship in which he "compared Reagan's willingness to see Volcker go to the decision by Kaiser Wilhelm II to dismiss Bismarck."[17]

One of the main problems with Volcker's approach was that it took a very long time (relatively speaking) to produce the intended effect. For more than two years, he tightened the money supply and strangled the economy. This indicates how much excess cash was in the system. It was one of the reasons for the systemic inflation – as hard to kill and tenacious as a cockroach. But eventually, persistence and patience paid off. As tough as it was on ordinary Americans, who saw their livelihoods affected in severe and unpredictable ways, this act of squeezing off the money supply set up the US economy for one of the longest and healthiest expansions in American history. During the latter half of the 1980s and through the 1990s, the United States enjoyed one of the most dynamic and prosperous times it ever had.

What was so amazing about Volcker's success against inflation is that, once he broke its hold on the US economy, the change in inflation and inflationary expectations was dramatic.[18] In 1981, inflation was running at more than 10%: however, by the end of 1982, it was less than 4% (in December 1982, inflation was 3.83%).[19] His restrictive monetary policy caused a significant recession in 1981–1982, with an unemployment rate that reached as high as 10.8%, but in the end it was worth the short-term pain for the long-term gain.[20] With inflation fears gone and the inflation beast conquered, the next phase of the inflation cycle occurred – the long and slow descent into deflation.

Chapter 2.
The Great Depression

Deflation is the opposite of inflation – consumers and producers believe that the price of a product today is higher than the price that the same product will be tomorrow. This makes consumers hesitant to purchase, because they know that same product will be available at a lower price at a future date. And it makes producers want to minimize their inventory, so that the value of their product is not decreasing while it sits on a shelf. This introduces a lag in the production line for more products, if those products suddenly experience a surge in demand.

We have all seen the effects of deflation – or falling prices – with respect to technology products, particularly in computer prices. Computer hardware and peripherals (personal computers, laptops, monitors, etc.) keep getting less expensive each year. Not long ago, the average price of a PC was about $3,000.[21] Today, you can purchase a much more capable computer with more memory and faster graphics for less than $1,000. With the velocity of change and improvement in speed and capability, today's product could be outdated in six months. Now the consumer is faced with the following dilemma: buy today and get locked into a product that could be obsolete in six months, or wait six months for that same product to cost half as much. Not long ago, some of the most humorous commercials on television were from the different mobile phone service providers that offer new plans for upgrading your phone "when you want" – as opposed to being locked into a two-year upgrade plan.

Deflation has a tendency to be self-perpetuating, similar to the wage-price spiral for inflation. As prices decline, producers make less of a product and may end up laying off workers. As unemployment rises, fewer consumers are able to purchase products, and aggregate demand falls. As demand falls, prices then fall lower, in keeping with the supply-demand curve. Unless there is a significant event or government involvement to provide relief via an economic stimulus package or by increasing employment in the government sector, the above scenario can become self-sustaining – to the detriment of all.

EXTREME DEFLATION - THE GREAT DEPRESSION

The Great Depression started soon after the collapse of the stock market in October 1929. That occurred many years before I was born; however, it was an event that severely influenced both my parents, and their stories of that era still linger in my memory (although, I can honestly say it didn't have the same effect on me as it had on them – for example, I don't feel compelled to eat everything on my plate, even though my parents always did). I can't imagine today suffering the same lack of basic necessities that my parents did. They didn't have many possessions and went hungry some days, but they actually led a life not much different than that of most people during the Depression.

The Great Depression began after the stock market crash in 1929, lasted throughout the 1930s, and ended at the start of World War II.[22] The severity of the downturn was actually made worse by the action (or inaction) of President Hoover and Congress. The Smoot-Hawley Act imposed severe tariffs on products shipped to the United States. The thinking was that this "protectionist" act would save US jobs, when actually the opposite occurred. By increasing tariffs and limiting imports, the US incited reactionary tariffs from other countries, thereby reducing sales of US products overseas.[23] This led to a slowdown in production and subsequent layoffs at exporting companies.

Another action taken by President Hoover that worsened conditions leading to the Great Depression was a tax cut he proposed at the end of 1929. In and of itself, the tax cut would not have caused much damage. However, President Hoover was also a champion of a balanced budget. He even urged the incoming president, Franklin Roosevelt, to maintain a balanced budget. By reducing revenues via the tax cut, he was also required to reduce spending at a time when additional federal spending was warranted.

The fear of going off the gold standard and risking inflation also made things worse. The country had experienced significant inflation over the prior decade, and all the financial advisors and economic policy experts were "looking in the rearview mirror," concerned about additional inflationary effects, when in fact the opposite was the case – the country was experiencing the worst deflation since the post-Civil War period. "The fear of inflation reinforced the demand for the balanced budget."[24]

Before the Great Depression started, unemployment was running at about 3%. By the time it was in full swing, unemployment peaked at about 25%.[25] This means that 15 million Americans were jobless. In part, the increase in unemployment was driven by a reduction in production, which itself was driven by a reduction in consumption. Former Fed Chair Ben Bernanke studied the Great Depression and has written extensively about it. He finds that tight monetary policy was the cause of the Great Depression.

Bernanke states that the Fed started raising the interest rate in 1928 through the recession that started in August 1929 and that this is what caused the stock market crash.[26] Then, liquidity issues arose as speculators purchased gold as a hedge, driving the dollar down and causing the Fed to again raise interest rates to compensate for the lowered dollar value. As the money supply tightened, it became more difficult to borrow money, and loans also cost more, due to the higher interest rates. This led more companies to go into default or bankruptcy, which then caused further unemployment.

During the Great Depression, more than 32,000 businesses went bankrupt and more than 5,000 banks failed. Wages dropped by 42%, prices fell by 10% per year, and GDP nearly halved (from $103 billion to $55 billion).[27] Farm prices dropped so low that most of the independent farmers went bankrupt or lost their farms to the bank. In addition, weather patterns in that decade provided record droughts, and the Midwest became a "dust bowl" – unable to sustain any crops whatsoever. As a result, many American farmers moved west, to California, in search of work. The great book by John Steinbeck, *The Grapes of Wrath*, fictionalized the stories of some of these people.[28]

Many books have been written and movies made about that terrible period in US history. The data and statistics are stark and revealing. As mentioned, tens of thousands of businesses went under, thousands of banks failed, and millions of people were out of work. Individuals moved around the country like migrant workers, looking for jobs. Whole families were torn apart by the Depression – people lost their homes when they couldn't pay the mortgage, farmers lost their farms and their way of life, men and women from all walks of life were affected. These were truly some of the darkest hours in American history.

OTHER DEFLATIONARY PERIODS

Interestingly, the Kondratieff cycle (to be defined later in this section) prior to the Great Depression also had its own significant deflationary period. The Gilded Age, from about 1870 to about 1900, was a time of corruption, extravagance, and greed. It also was the most recent depressionary era prior to the 1930s. What is known as the "Long Depression" lasted from 1873 to 1879 and was the country's most severe prior to the Great Depression. In fact, per the National Bureau of Economic Research (NBER), the Long Depression's peak-to-trough cycle was actually longer than the Great Depression's peak-to-trough cycle (65 months versus 43 months).[29]

It is also interesting to note that, according to NBER data, the average expansion cycle is longer than the average contraction cycle, or recession. Data on the NBER website show the average expansion to be 38.7 months and the average contraction to be 17.5 months. These numbers have been trending longer for the past several cycles.

In May 2002, I attended a lecture series featuring Todd Buchholz. Todd is a noted economist and writer, and I had read two of his books, *Market Shock* and *New Ideas from Dead Economists*. After his lecture, I asked him what he thought about the prospect of deflation in the coming years. He seemed surprised by the question. I don't think he thought it was likely, or maybe the question caught him off guard. But at the time, I thought the prospects were real. It seemed to me that the prices for products like consumer electronics, tools, and most major goods shipped from China and sold in the US were much less than they were in prior years.

In November 2002, Fed Chair Ben Bernanke gave a speech on deflation in Richmond, Virginia. What is significant about this event is that it signaled a shift in Fed focus, from an inflation-fighting stance to a deflation-fighting posture.[30] His concerns could have been caused by Great Depression-type fears, due to the stock market collapse of 2000–2003 (including the effects of 9/11). However, I believe that the tax law act of 2001, which pumped $1.3 trillion in revenue back into the US economy (over a period of 10 years, at about $130 billion per year), prevented the economic collapse that Bernanke and the Fed feared.

Jason Zweig writes in his commentary on Benjamin Graham's *The Intelligent Investor*, "…the annual rise in the cost of goods and services averaged less than 2.2% between 1997 and 2002 – and economists believe that even that rock-bottom rate may be overstated."[31] His commentary, published in 2003, further implies that deflation is a real possibility and causes investors more concern than inflation. "When inflation is highly negative … stocks do very poorly."[32]

Interest rates are currently at their lowest since the early 1960s – that's more than 50 years. What drove interest rates so low back then is also what is driving interest rates low now – the availability of cheap products holding prices down across the economy. Interest rates are a reflection of inflation. Typically, the inflation rate reflects the interest rate, in that, as inflation goes lower, so does the interest rate. This is known as "Gibson's paradox." Back in the early 1960s, Japan was providing thousands of inexpensive products across a wide range, from electronics to automobiles. We are reliving that experience now, with China providing everything from steel to electronics to household items at a fraction of the cost of American-made counterparts. This is a benefit to consumers, but it puts a lot of pressure on producers to become more cost-competitive.

MOORE'S LAW AND DEFLATION

The prices of consumer goods, especially electronics and computer-related products, have been falling in relative terms for the last couple of decades. Technology has driven much of that cost reduction, through automation (removing the expensive human labor component of product prices); increases in efficiency (by using computers to minimize work flow costs, touch labor, and inventory); and the Internet (the reduction and/or elimination of distribution costs by selling directly to the consumer). All these effects have put downward pressure on product prices, at least for those types of products that can maximize these cost efficiencies.

A well-known law in computer technology, Moore's Law, explains some of the effects of technology on product prices. Moore's Law states that the number of transistors on an integrated circuit (IC) doubles every two years. This translates to a 2X factor in the capability of the semiconductor-based IC (used in microprocessors). This effectively cuts in half the cost of an equivalent product every two years. You can always buy last year's product for less than you did the year before, thus reducing the price of every microprocessor-based product in inventory.

We are also seeing asset prices, in terms of real estate, fall from their peak in 2006 to half, and in some areas, less than half of what they were at the peak. The recent real estate bubble and the popping of asset prices will be discussed at greater length in a subsequent chapter, but it is another contributor to the deflation occurring at the end of the current Kondratieff wave. The Fed kept interest rates artificially low by purchasing billions of dollars worth of bonds, in an effort to fight deflation by boosting real estate prices. As long as interest rates are 4% and below, asset prices in real estate should be able to recover and regain some of their losses from the trillion-dollar meltdown of 2006–2009.

Former Fed Chair Ben Bernanke's speech in July 2013 stated that because of the "constraint posed by the effective lower bound on short-term interest rates" (the federal funds rate has been at or near zero since 2008), the Fed has been able to "respond to economic developments" (fight deflation) by affecting interest rates "further out on the yield curve" (long-term interest rates).[33] What the Fed has done is purchase $85 billion worth of securities monthly ($40 billion in agency mortgage-backed securities and $45 billion in Treasuries) over a long time period (from September 2012 to the end of 2013, tapering off to zero by October 2014) to maintain economic stability and asset prices.

JAPAN AND DEFLATION

Japan is a model for how not to handle the slide into deflation. Authorities there were too slow to react to the bursting of the country's own asset bubbles in real estate and the equities market in the late 1980s and early 1990s, and even though interest rates jumped from 2.5% to 6% in just over a year in 1991, the Japanese still were hesitant to lay off workers or reduce production capacity.[34] Japan tried to use exports as a vehicle to lead it out of its recession; however, it was an uphill battle, because of the effects of excess worldwide manufacturing capacity, the overcapitalization of plants and equipment, high labor costs, and low interest rates.

The Plaza Accord was an agreement between several nations "...to intervene in the foreign exchange markets to depreciate the dollar. The agreement took its name from the Plaza Hotel, a New York City landmark overlooking Central Park."[35] In addition, the Plaza Accord in 1985 drove the US dollar down relative to the yen, which provided for a healthy recovery of US manufacturing capability; however, it caused additional stress to the Japanese economy, as exports were increasingly costlier with respect to US prices. The combination of these effects caused the Japanese to suffer a long and drawn-out recession and deflation in their prices.

From the 1980s to the year 2000, there was a decline in worldwide manufacturing profitability. This was due to the competitiveness factors and labor costs of competing manufacturing countries in the Far East. It was also affected by the effect of the currency exchange rates between the US and other countries. Since the year 2000, the China effect has driven the prices of manufactured products even lower. Now, China's refusal to raise its currency valuation relative to other countries has held down its prices artificially, and like the Reverse Plaza Accord of 1995, it is driving the prices of manufactured goods ever lower.

The Reverse Plaza Accord was put in place to save the Japanese economy from a complete meltdown and to allow the manufacturing and export economy to recover its 1980s form, or at least some semblance of its prior glory.[36] The accord also allowed both the German and Japanese governments to direct investment flows into the US economy. This helped stabilize economic conditions in both Japan and Germany, but once again drove down the price of imported manufactured products in the US, a condition that became more apparent when China launched its export-led economic recovery in the 2000s.

GLOBALIZATION AND DEFLATION

Global competition and current economic conditions have driven unemployment rates up and held wages down for quite some time now. The "wage gap" difference between productivity increases and salaries has been increasing for the past 20 years or more. This process can't go on forever. As producers search the world for employees who will perform labor at the lowest rates, there will be a point where the means does not justify the ends. At some point, there will be a turnaround, as the economy and the supply and demand curves fall to equilibrium.

The cycle will turn around as the wages of employees making these products eventually rise to force an increase in product pricing. In addition, the number of consumers in China now able to purchase some of the goods they produce will increase demand for these products, shifting the aggregate demand curve and driving prices higher. Globalization will eventually reduce the deflationary effects of cheap labor, as the awareness and desire for the latest technological product increases aggregate demand to the point of an inflationary effect.

While the US economy has successfully averted an economic depression and only suffered the worst recession in the past 50 years – the Great Recession, as it is called in the media – the swing of the pendulum back into an inflationary period will not be without its challenges, pain, and suffering. The effects of inflation are far-reaching and affect everyone. Inflation creates uncertainty and angst, as nobody knows how, when, or even if it will end (except those of you reading this book). Inflation has a tendency to cause people to give up hope in the future and "live for today." This leads to high rates of debt leveraging and lower savings rates. It increases consumption and further increases inflation, as people try to spend now in order to consume and convert their spending power into tangible assets and products.

Chapter 3.
The Kondratieff (Inflation) Cycle

Inflation runs in a 54-year cycle known as the Kondratieff cycle, or the "Long Wave," which represents the changes in prices of products over time. I first became aware of the Kondratieff cycle when I was doing a paper for my macroeconomics class during my MBA years. It was 1998, and I was intrigued by the stock market and wondering if it was a bubble. I was looking at long-term cycles, and I was thinking that there had to be a reason why the market was going up. I just didn't understand, at that point, that it wasn't related to the Long Wave cycle.

Nikolai Kondratieff, a Russian economist of the 1920s, wrote several papers dealing with the question of long economic cycles. In his book, aptly titled *Long Economic Cycles*, he showed how several indices, such as commodity prices, interest rates, wages, and foreign trade, vary over time. From this data, a consistent and repeatable form emerged – a cyclical pattern of consistent length. This curve came to be known as the Kondratieff wave. This curve can be compared to the actual values of these indices over long periods of time and is shown to be predictive. If you take the curve for commodity prices or interest rates and project it out for the last 100 years (which is actually only two long cycles), it is surprisingly accurate (see Figure 5). This figure is from Dewey and Dakin's *Cycles: The Science of Prediction*. In 1947, when this book was published, the authors predicted a peak in wholesale prices in the early 1980s – and that is exactly what happened. Prices topped out in 1982, at the peak of the Great Inflation, and they have been on a downward slope since then.

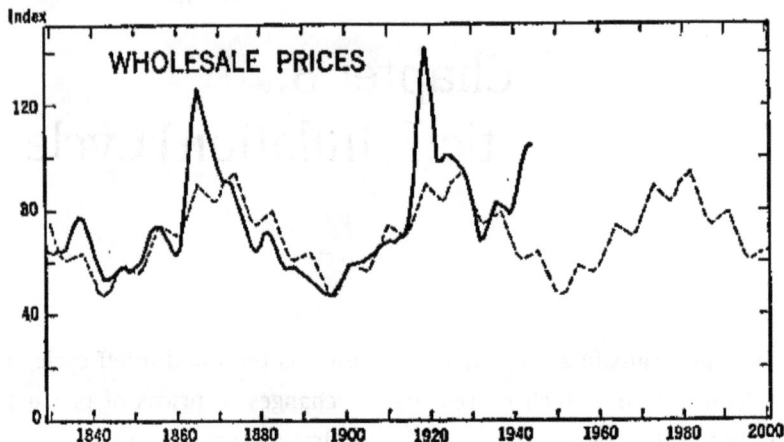

Figure 5. The Kondratieff Cycle Price Predictor[37]

The Kondratieff Wave is shown in Figure 6.[38] Inflation is associated with the "up" wave of the Kondratieff cycle. It coincides with wars, which cause the economy to overproduce to keep up with demand. In addition, the government usually prints excessive amounts of money in order to pay for the war. From there, aggregate demand takes over, followed by the wage-price cycle. Deflation is then associated with the "down" wave of the cycle – note the deflationary periods following the financial panics of 1873 and 1929.

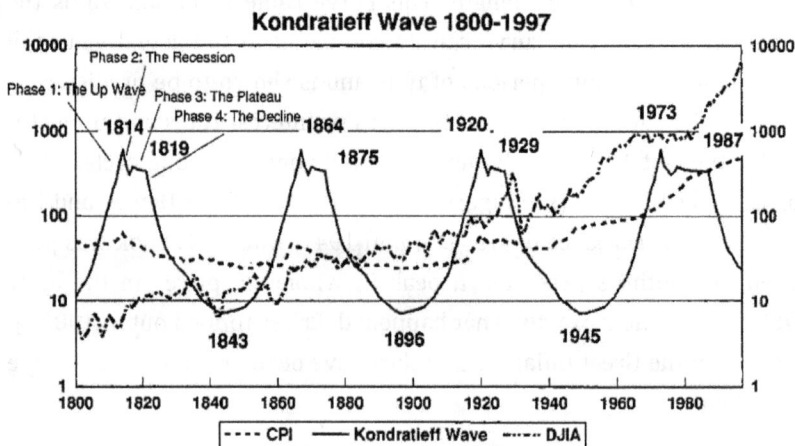

Figure 6. The Kondratieff Cycle (courtesy of A. Gary Shilling & Co, Inc)

THE KONDRATIEFF WAVE AND TECHNOLOGY

Kondratieff noted four empirical patterns in the long wave that are described in his book *Long Economic Cycles*. The first pattern has to do with technological change and the initial development and experimentation of a new idea or invention, which is associated with the upward phase of the cycle. The second pattern has to do with the competition of resources due to the technological change and the conflicts or wars over those resources. In addition, there is social unrest or upheaval caused by the technological change and this pattern is also associated with the upward phase of the cycle. The third pattern is that there is a significant reduction in agricultural and commodity prices associated with the initial downward phase of the long cycle. The fourth pattern that Kondratieff identified is that the downward phase of the long cycle is associated with depression or deflation.[39]

The Long Wave has been associated with other aspects besides inflation or deflation. In addition, the Long Wave is related to periods of technological change. As new technology advances are assimilated into the mainstream, they change how things are done and how people implement and get used to these advances. The figure above represents four waves of technological innovation. The earlier technology advances were associated with transportation and the speed of travel (including the speed of movement of goods and services). These advances were the steam engine, which became the basis for land (locomotive) and sea (steamship) travel. The next advance was the gasoline engine, which was smaller and more portable, making it capable of being used in smaller vehicles, such as the automobile.

In the United States, we have seen several technological waves of innovation and advancement. In the early years of US history, it was all about steam power. From about 1789 until about 1842, steamboats were everywhere up and down the Mississippi River, and other steam-powered machines ruled the day. This transitioned to railroads in 1843–1897, as industrialists and capitalists poured tons of resources (mainly steel) into the development of a network of railroads and the systems to support it. Railroads gave way to the automobile and the internal combustion engine – which also sparked the airplane industry – from 1897 to 1952. Then the transistor was invented, and the electronic/computer age was born.

This advance was in keeping with things getting smaller – from steam engines to gasoline engines to the transistor. Developments in transistor design were transformed by the invention of the semiconductor transistor, which occurred in the 1950s – the Shockley transistor is named for William Shockley, who worked at Bell Labs. The semiconductor transistor went on to become the basis for the computer, and the information age had arrived. From 1952 until 2006, the computer and digital technology (also known as information technology) age has dominated the economic scene. So, we went from the speed of travel to the speed of information. And since the speed of information is the speed of electricity, we are talking about the speed of light.

The invention of the semiconductor is the driving force behind the wave of technological innovation driving the worldwide economy for more than 50 years. Since that is the span of a full Kondratieff wave, I believe we are close to the next technological revolution that will affect our future. It is possible that the new technology has already been invented, and we are on the path to our next wave of change. It is widely believed that the next technological wave will probably come from the nanotechnology or biotechnology fields.

THE NEXT TECHNOLOGY WAVE

What will the next technological advance bring us? What will be the "creative destruction" forces that drive investment and other resources into its creation and evolution? Light may be that next area of transformation. Because the next crisis is going to be related to energy and the ability to produce oil, I believe this upcoming invention or transformation will have something to do with the sun and/or solar energy. Solar energy is plentiful, it is cheap (free), it is ecologically responsible, and it is renewable. The limits to solar energy are battery technology (storage) and capacity (silicon board density). Solar energy is not the most efficient energy transfer, but it is by far the most democratic – the sun is shining everywhere all the time (within the limits of weather and the time of day). The Advanced Research Projects Agency – Energy (ARPA-E) is just the type of government agency that could come up with the next Kondratieff wave-level invention or idea, like the Bell Labs Shockley transistor invention. ARPA-E is modeled after DARPA (the Defense Advanced Research Projects Agency), "...the legendary Pentagon agency that fathered the Internet and GPS technology."[40]

Whatever the case may be, I believe that the coming technological change or invention that will drive the next Kondratieff wave will be related to energy. As we suffer the end result of our dependency on fossil fuels, the prices of all petroleum-based products will skyrocket as inflation soars. As the weather changes – caused by the increase in greenhouse gases, which raises the temperature of our oceans and melts the polar ice caps – millions of lives will be impacted. As the rise in the ocean levels devours millions of miles of coastlines, and tidewaters reach farther and farther inland, millions of people will be forced to move. I hope technology will soon provide an answer to the question of how we can obtain our energy independence and harness a renewable energy source to eliminate our dependence on fossil fuels.

The next major invention or technological change related to energy will be a game changer. This invention, or inventions, will provide relief in various areas of consumer life in terms of a reduction in our reliance on fossil fuels, which in turn lessens air pollution, increases air quality, improves health, builds financial stability, and solves world hunger. Well, solving world hunger may be going a little too far, but we do need to find a solution to the energy problem.

INTEREST RATES AND INFLATION

Finally, there is a third aspect of the Long Wave that should be discussed – interest rates. In fact, I originally called this "the interest rates chapter." Inflation and interest rates are highly correlated. If it can be assumed that inflation is related to the prices of goods and services, as in "wholesale prices," then it has been demonstrated that inflation and interest rates move together in rhythm with a period equivalent to the

Kondratieff wave. This is known as "Gibson's Paradox," as related by Keynes, and described by Kondratieff in his treatise "Long Economic Cycles" (as translated by Guy Daniels in *The Long Wave Cycle*).[41]

Interest rates are used as a lever to control inflation. Controlled inflation is actually considered a good thing by most economists. Milton Friedman stated that "...the crucial function of a central bank is to produce price stability, interpreted as a low and relatively steady recorded rate of inflation."[42] The Fed will increase the federal funds rate (the rate at which banks can borrow money from the government and which provides a base rate from which other rates are calculated) when it wants to "slow down" the economy in order to rein in inflation. However, the Fed will also decrease the federal funds rate to spur the economy and avoid a recession, or to attempt to bring the country out of a recession. For example, since the Great Recession of 2007–2009, the Fed has brought down the federal funds rate to nearly 0%. This has held interest rates to their lowest levels in 50 years and prompted speculation that inflation could creep back into the economy (which it will, as you will soon see).

Questions about inflation and interest rates dogged Fed Chairman Bernanke since the stimulus package implementation in 2008. As late as September 2012, Bernanke defended Fed policies on the stimulus package and how they addressed the sluggish economy. His testimony to Congress in July 2013 sheds light on his view of inflation: "...the Committee would be likely to view a decline in unemployment to 6-1/2 percent as a sufficient reason to raise its target for the federal funds rate."[43]

The great Fed Chairman Bill Martin was quoted as saying his job was to "take away the punch bowl, just as the party is getting good."[44] What he was referring to is that the Fed has to predict when to react to mounting inflationary pressures and take those measures before the long-term trends can be established. The Fed has to balance the short-term business needs for growth and low-cost access to capital, and the public needs for employment opportunities, against the long-term effects of low interest rates that could cause overinvestment and overstimulation of the economy and long-term damage in terms of inflation.

OTHER FACTORS DRIVING INFLATION

An expectation of higher prices will also affect inflation. In the 1970s, prices kept increasing due to an overstimulation of the economy. This caused unions to demand higher wages to counter the effects of that inflation. Higher wages led to higher costs of production, which caused many industries to increase the prices of their products to maintain a profit margin. The results of the higher product prices led to additional demands for higher pay, resulting in a wage-price spiral.

The Long Wave should also be considered when thinking about the global effects of change. As businesses and economies become more interconnected and integrated in all industries, the "butterfly effect" should be considered: What seems like a small and simple thing could have huge effects if leveraged over multiple years or hundreds of thousands of business decisions. And since the Kondratieff wave is so long and takes so many years to fully develop, the changes introduced or forced upon the public by these events can have unforeseen and unintended consequences. For example, a replacement technology for the reciprocating engine, due to some advance in fuel, power, or energy, could completely disrupt the current auto industry and put multiple thousands of people out of work. Depending on the type of advance, it could be hundreds of thousands. This would have a significant effect on the economy.

What we have always relied on, is that technology will come to our aid. What is needed now are the technological solutions to our growing problems: pollution of our lakes and rivers, global warming due to excess greenhouse gases in our atmosphere, rising sea levels due to the melting of the polar caps, and extreme weather affecting the lives of hundreds of thousands of people. Extreme weather in the United States includes: severe tornados in the Midwest, hurricanes in the Southeast and on the East Coast, and droughts and floods in the West. Technology can and should help us understand and solve these complex problems.

Other effects of severe weather are the displacement of populations and the long-term impacts on farming and food production. The worldwide effects of new weather patterns will be felt mostly in agriculture, as the world's arable land is reduced, due to rising oceans and decreasing rainfall. *The Los Angeles Times* reported on February 22, 2013, that most of the western United States faces drought conditions that will affect most of the US's cattle lands.[45] This is another example of climate change affecting our weather patterns. Changes in food production levels will occur at the same time that demand will increase, due to population growth. This will drive prices and inflation ever upward.

Transportation costs will become a huge factor in product costs, and those costs will be passed on to the consumer. The Mississippi River has also been affected by the drought. "All along the lower Mississippi – from Memphis, Tenn., to New Orleans – water levels are at record lows."[46] If this waterway gets shut down by drought, alternative methods of transporting grain, soybeans, and other food products could cost three to four times as much, increasing the products' end prices. Gas and diesel fuel costs will also drive up food prices. As fuel costs increase, this transportation cost will also be passed through to the consumer. This will make local farmers' markets and, quite potentially, street vendors much more competitive with respect to the prices of products in wholesale markets.

In addition to transportation costs, the costs of energy will dominate production, as every British Thermal Unit (BTU) of energy used in heating or cooling a factory, lighting an office, and providing power to computer terminals, phone systems, and the like will cost more. This will drive the costs of production as much as any other single input. The other input that will eventually drive cost will be labor. As salaries increase due to the wage-price spiral, those expenses will also end up in the bottom-line price of products. The wage-price spiral significantly affected the cost of products during the last inflationary period in the 1970s.

As the last inflationary period taught us, money supply will be a significant factor in controlling inflation. It remains to be seen if the expected oil shock caused by declining worldwide oil production will be the motivating factor in the overall price of products going forward, but I believe it will. Oil and other natural resources will undergo a significant increase in aggregate demand, due to the continued industrialization of the BRIC (Brazil, Russia, India, and China) nations. In addition, the worldwide increases in global wealth, especially the surges in the number of middle-income populations, will increase consumption and force prices higher.

THE END OF MOORE'S LAW

The final nail in the deflation coffin that will eventually turn that curve upside down will be the end of Moore's law. At some point, there is a physical limit to the number of circuits you can put on the head of a pin. The computer industry will eventually reach that limit, and when they do, there will no longer be that self-perpetuating reduction in the price of computer products or increase in the performance thereof. As the computer industry has gone from one technology to another (light stencil, ultraviolet, x-rays, electron beams – and now 3D) to increase the volume and accuracy of increased circuitry, we are getting closer to the physical limit, and at that point, there will be no material ability to condense more memory per unit of area. That is, we will have reached the end of the line for this low-hanging-fruit technology driver for smaller and cheaper products.

Because of the long length of the inflationary cycle, people have a hard time relating to it. It takes more than a generation for the down cycle, when prices are declining, and people think that inflation has gone away. "So strong was the decline of prices by 1996 that several leading economists asserted that the age of inflation was at an end."[47] However, this is just the typical rear-view-mirror perspective of any person who is trying to predict the future by extrapolating the recent past. It does not work. Everything in life has a cycle, and the next phase of Kondratieff's Long Wave will be the upswing of the inflation cycle.

Chapter 4.
What's Next for Inflation

What will we see in the future, relative to inflation? If you look at the 54-year cycle of US wholesale prices in Figure 5, taken from *Cycles: The Science of Prediction* by Dewey and Dakin, you can see the peak corresponds to the peak of the last major inflation wave in 1982.[48] Since this book was published in 1947, it is amazing to me how accurate that prediction was. And since 1982, there has been a reduction in prices, per the predictive curve. In fact, "... the rate of price inflation has been falling on average for 27 years."[49] This also tells me that the lowest point in prices (deflation) should have been in 2009 and that the next peak in the prices of products (inflation) will be in 2036.

The question is, what is going to spur that change? What will cause the deflationary pressures of low-cost products, logistical efficiencies, information technology, and low labor costs to reverse, so that inflation can start its eventual rise? The answer is – oil. The worldwide production of oil will peak this decade, after which there will be less and less of it pumped from the ground. Oil is the major lubricant of the economy. There are so many products that are petrochemical-based that it would be difficult to imagine our society running on anything else. At some point, we will have to not just imagine it but plan for it, and that transition will be long, difficult, and costly.

There is a well-known prediction called "Hubbert's Peak," which relates to the declining rate at which oil would be produced from wells within the United States. M. King Hubbert, a Shell Oil geophysicist, forecasted in the 1950s that this would occur around 1970. He was correct. What we found out from the oil crisis in 1973 was that the US could no longer simply increase the production of domestic oil to offset the reduction in the availability of foreign oil. Since then. we have been affected by price-setting by the Middle East oil cartels.

HUBBARD'S PEAK AND INFLATION

What will happen when the worldwide Hubbert's Peak occurs? In *Out of Gas*, David Goodstein states: "One certain effect will be steep inflation, because gasoline, along with everything made from petrochemicals and everything that has to be transported, will suddenly cost more."[50] As I stated above in the opening paragraph on inflation, an oil shock is the only thing necessary to replicate the conditions of the last inflationary episode in our nation's history, the Great Inflation. I expect this oil shock to occur this decade, and the repercussions will be severe. At some point in the near future, we will reach the worldwide peak production of oil. After this date, any global event that requires a surge of additional oil reserves to compensate – whether that be a war, a natural disaster, a collusion of oil-producing countries cutting total output, or some other cause – will reveal that there will be no way to react to that need, and hence there will be an oil shock.

The result of this oil shock will be a repeat of the 1970s OPEC oil embargo. The US will suffer long lines at the gas pump, prices of products that are shipped or driven anywhere will increase, and there will be a general unease with the state of the economy. In addition, there will be global shortages and price increases, because this will be a worldwide problem. Unlike the 1970s, this shortage will be due to the global Hubbert's Peak event, which will affect world oil production. In the 1970s, other countries, such as Venezuela and Nigeria, were producing oil at a rate that was offsetting the decrease in production in the OPEC nations; however, those other countries were not on good trading terms with the United States, and so their oil production did not benefit the US.

Hubbert's curve for oil production in the United States was based on an assumed Gaussian curve distribution and a total number of barrels produced. That estimate proved to be incredibly accurate. The total number of barrels of worldwide production is estimated at 2.1 trillion.[51] If that estimate is accurate, then we should have seen peak oil no later than 2009. Since that has not yet happened, then obviously the total estimate is wrong. However, there has been production from the United States and other countries from a new methodology called hydraulic fracturing, or fracking. This technique has led to an increase in oil production without having to engage in expensive drilling activities.

COMMODITIES AND INFLATION

Oil and gas are not the only commodities poised to raise global product prices. As Dambisa Moyo writes in her book *Winner Take All*, water, food, metals, and minerals are all commodities that will become more and more in demand because of global population growth and the increase in earning capacity and wealth of some of the world's most populous nations – China and India.[52] Changing weather patterns will cause more severe droughts in some areas and more extreme flooding in others. Also, weather systems will become more powerful and damaging to life and property. This will make potable water and food production much more strategic in the future, as arable lands become consumed by the rising oceans.

The current dispute between China and Japan over the Senkaku Islands in the East China Sea may have its roots in oil. International law provided ownership of ocean mineral, oil, and gas rights to countries based on ownership of the land in the vicinity (equidistant between neighboring countries), regardless of whether or not that land (or island) is inhabited.[53] China has announced an air defense zone (ADZ) around the Senkaku Islands, based on their claimed ownership of the islands (see Figure 7). The United States rejected the Chinese claim and flew unarmed B-52 bombers through the ADZ to show support for Japan's rights to the islands. Since the United Nations has identified potential oil and gas reserves around the Senkaku Islands, it is probable that this is a new claim by China in order to assert its rights to the oil found in the region.[54]

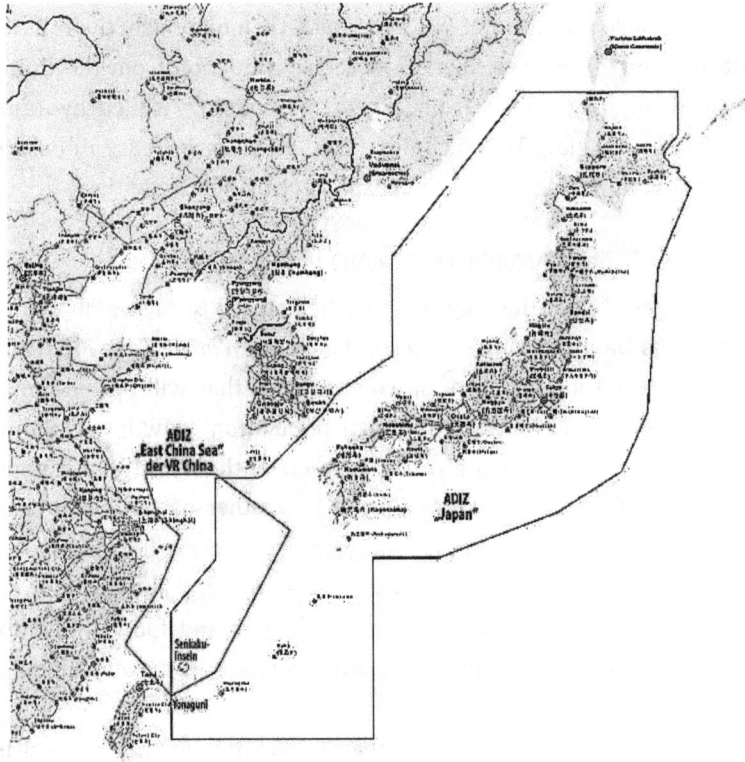

Figure 7. China vs. Japan Claim of the Senkaku Islands

The islands in the South China Sea are also contested among seven different countries for ownership rights. The Paracel Islands, which had been claimed in the early 19th century by Vietnam, and the Spratley Islands, which had been claimed by the Philippines, are now claimed by China as part of their overall control and ownership of the South China Seas. There are already several ocean oil drilling platforms in the region. The potential oil reserve estimates for this area are as high as over 200 billion barrels.[55]

Mineral deposits around the world have become acquisition targets for China. An article in *The Los Angeles Times* on March 24, 2013, documents a $3 billion agreement between a Chinese consortium and the Afghan government to develop a copper deposit in the Logar province of

Afghanistan.[56] A second article on the same date discusses the issues that Myanmar has with Chinese investments in that country, with indigenous demonstrations at a Chinese-backed copper mine and the suspension of a $3.6 billion Chinese-built hydroelectric project.[57]

CHINA AND INFLATION

Inflation will also be driven into the cost of the products produced in China, due to the increases in energy costs. Products are typically shipped to the United States in forty-foot shipping containers. As an example, consider the following scenario: "During the spring of 2008, with gas at $3.50, sending the container from China to the East Coast took $8,350. When gas approaches $5, getting the metal box to New York will run $10,000; when gas approaches $8 per gallon, the ocean freight for a container will run $15,000."[58] In essence, increases in energy costs act like a tax on products shipped overseas, whether from China or other countries.

As Chinese workers move up the productivity scale from low-paying, labor-intensive jobs to higher paying technical and skilled-labor jobs, they will move up the income curve. Blue-collar workers in China are seeking higher paying jobs in technical manufacturing and in the automotive industry. In addition, costs to produce manufactured products in China are increasing as much as 15% per year, driven by the costs of labor, energy, and raw materials.[59] Also, as Chinese workers move up the income curve, they will consume more of the products they produce. As demand increases, so will overall prices. This is an argument for inflation, which will occur for this and many other reasons.

China must allow the expansion of its economy or risk an even more dangerous situation – social unrest and upheaval. The threat is that the seeds of discontent have been sown in the Tiananmen Square event and the persecution of Chinese dissidents. The Chinese people are slowly waking up to the good life provided by a capitalistic society. The population and its slow evolution from a pure agrarian society to a manufacturing- and technology-based society will drive worldwide economic and political change. An article in *The Los Angeles Times* on April 26, 2011, stated that inflation in China was at almost a three-year high and was 5.4% higher than the prior year. It talked about a truckers' strike in Shanghai's largest port, which was being driven by high diesel prices and port fees. In the article, a professor from Renmin University in Beijing stated: "We call inflation over 5% 'vicious inflation'...It's the biggest threat to the government."[60]

China will soon have almost 400 million people that will have a median income equivalent to what defines a "middle class" – a prospect that is equally terrifying and amazingly impressive.[61] It is daunting to think of the pressure that a population of that magnitude puts on the world's ecosystems and economic ability to support that level of consumption. It is incredible to think how a centrally planned economy could have accomplished this in about three decades. Since the leadership of Premiers Zhao Ziyang and Li Ping, the socioeconomic growth and stability of the Chinese middle class has been steady and strong in both breadth and depth.

The creation of a Chinese middle class that is larger than the entire population of the United States will drive economic and political changes for years to come. Think of what the baby boom generation did to the US economy, and then project that forward to what the Chinese economy could do on a global scale. In fact, as the number of middle-class people in the global population grows, an exponential increase in the demand for higher end products, goods, and services will drive prices – due to the aggregate demand curve. Not only will aggregate demand drive prices, due to the supply/demand curve, it will also drive the consumption of raw materials and an increase in the cost of basic materials used to manufacture these new "standard of living" products. By this I mean, as everyone on the planet will soon want his or her own personal communication device, or smartphone, the rare minerals and raw materials used in the manufacture of these products will rise to the point of driving the base costs.

CHINA'S GROWTH AND LABOR SUPPLY

This is why so many US companies are attempting to establish a major presence in China. Growth drives most corporations' income, and income/revenue propels stock prices. All major corporations in the US and Europe are preparing for the economic boom times to come. These good times will be part of that driving force that will push the stock market, much like the baby boom generation that drove the stock market of the 1950s. No less an authority than the Oracle of Omaha, Warren Buffett, is championing this drive. He has travelled extensively to China and held meetings with several leading industrialists in that country. Buffett and his team have also had discussions with several prominent politicians there.[62]

In 2011, with inflation running at 5% (*The Los Angeles Times*, April 26, 2011), Chinese workers were poised to strike for higher pay in order to maintain their standard of living. Shanghai had a truckers' strike in April of that year, and this was after a Chinese New Year holiday celebration in which many businesses were concerned about the return of local farm workers to their jobs.

The lack of an adequate supply of workers will also force up labor costs, as supply and demand take effect. Skilled workers, especially those with technological experience and knowledge, will be greatly in demand, and there will be an increasing dividend paid to those workers with the right education. In addition, there will be a growing income spread between the "haves" with the right background and education versus those "have nots" who are manual laborers or uneducated/unskilled workers.

As I have already discussed, oil and all oil-based products will lead the upward movement in prices. The increases in costs for oil will be followed by surges in the prices of commodities of all kinds: gold, platinum, and other minerals, agricultural and food products, and ultimately, real estate. Wages will have to rise, as workers will demand higher incomes to pay for the increases across the board. Then, as expenses rise (labor is usually the highest cost element of a product), so will begin the wage-price spiral. These spiraling costs will drive the overall upward movement in product prices and cause significant economic challenges for politicians and labor leaders alike. There has already been a speculative boom in farm acreage real estate prices. I was on a flight from Cedar Rapids, Iowa, back to my home in Los Angeles, when I met a real estate investor and speculator. He was telling me about friends of his who were buying acres of farmland, expecting the prices of commodities to increase and to propel the prices of farmland with them.

CONSUMER CONFIDENCE AND INFLATION

There are other by-products of inflation. Inflation has a tendency to negatively impact people's impressions of economic conditions. It has the effect of taking away the stability of the future and makes people want to spend what they have now, because they won't be able to buy the same amount of goods in the future – inflation robs people of their hope. It will reduce the overall worldwide savings rate, as individuals will spend today what they don't think will have value tomorrow. It will also add to the commodities rush as people invest in hard assets, because all paper assets will lose more value over time. The commodities rush is already occurring, as already stated, and that will only increase over time. What is currently dampening the "gold rush" for hard assets is the cost of holding commodities for long periods of time. Once that drag on the demand curve is mitigated, I predict that gold prices will rise like a helium balloon on a warm summer day.

Kenneth S. Deffeyes states in his book *Hubbert's Peak: The Impending World Oil Shortage*, "I taught at Princeton from 1967 to 1997; faculty morale was at its lowest in the years around 1980. Inflation was raising the cost of living far faster than salaries increased."[63] He goes on to say, "Our real standard of living went progressively lower for several years in a row. That was life (with tenure) inside the sheltered ivory tower; outside it was much tougher."[64] And it will be that way again. People will become depressed. They will lose hope. They will feel as if there is no way they will come out of the situation they are in. It will take some time, but we will eventually get there. Inflation has a way of sneaking up on people. At first, they don't seem to notice. Then it gains momentum and becomes an all-consuming monster.

CRIME AND INFLATION

The other significant impact inflation has is on crime. Crime increases as inflation increases. You can see this in Figure 8, Homicides in Los Angeles. It was on the front page of *The Los Angeles Times* while I was researching topics for this book. Notice how the number increases from the 1960s (low inflation), then peaks in the 1980s (high inflation), and then is low again in the current time period (another low inflation era). This is not unique to Los Angeles. As you can see in Figure 9 (from *The Great Wave*, by Fischer), a similar effect is generalized for the United States. Note that the curves in Figure 9 show rates of theft and homicide per 100,000 population. You can expect the homicide rate to again increase as inflation rises over the next 15–20 years. I understand that this is not a desirable effect or outcome; however, the trending data show that this could potentially become the case.

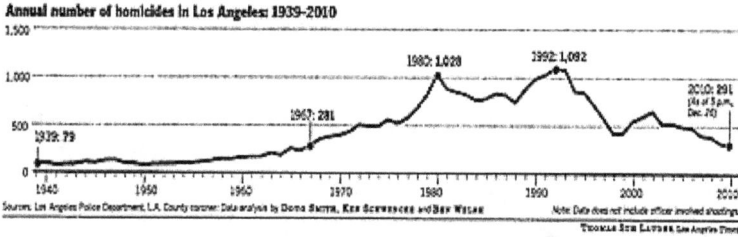

Figure 8. Homicides in Los Angeles[65]

The Price Revolution of the Twentieth Century
Crime and Consumer Prices in the United States, 1965-1995

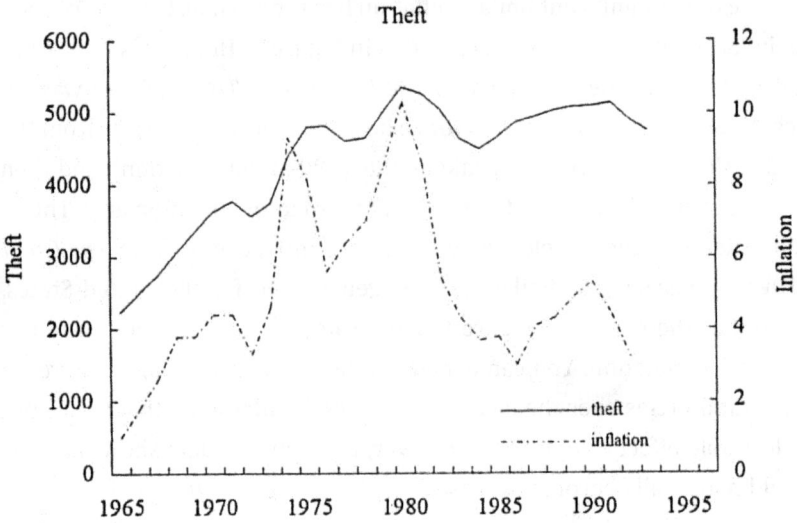

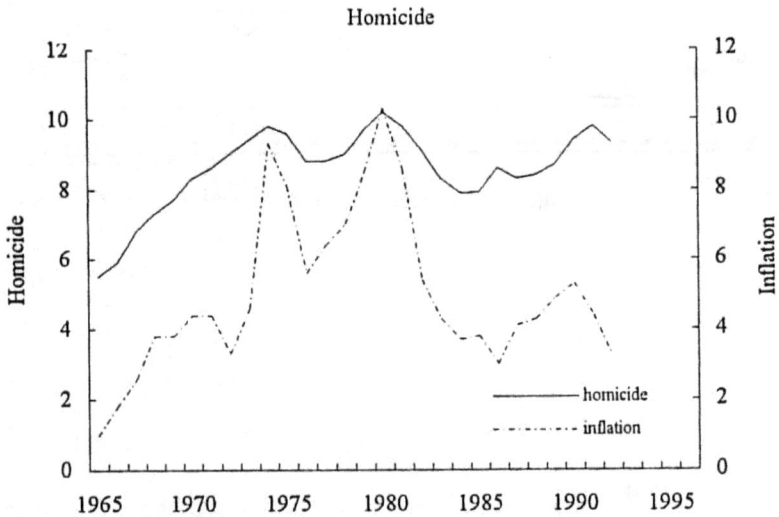

Figure 9. Theft and Homicides in the United States[66]

The Stock Market

The stock market craze of the 1990s, followed by the crash of 2000, was not a bubble. Valuations of companies are what drive the stock market. These valuations are based on quarterly income statements, the actual earnings from the current quarter and the projected earnings for the next quarter. Wall Street analysts then process these data to project 1-, 3-, 5-, and 10-year estimates of future value, or future profits, and this is what determines a stock's valuation. You can use any number of methodologies to predict this value, and there is a whole industry dedicated to the determination of this number and the (usually) quarterly updates to it. Since the projection of current earnings is what a company valuation is based on, all companies are subject to pressures to maintain or increase earnings. From that, the market will determine what the ultimate price is for a company.

The reason I don't believe the stock market of the late 1990s was a bubble is because, as an engineer working in the aerospace industry, I saw firsthand what was propelling it. Technology companies were all the rage, because their profits, quarter over quarter and year over year, kept going up. There seemed no end to the boom. Everyone was heavily investing in hardware and software, and in software consulting. Then, the tech-heavy NASDAQ fell from over 5,000 to less than 2,000 – a greater than 60% decline – in less than six months. Why? The answer is Y2K.

Chapter 5.
Y2K and the 1990s Boom

The boom phase of the millennial stock market actually started with President George H.W. Bush's commitment to slow the growing federal deficit by raising taxes. Although this may have doomed his re-election campaign, it put in place the parameters that President Bill Clinton would use in his deficit reduction plan. The stock market hit 3,000 in 1991, and from that point on, the steady and consistent march through 1,000-point barriers for the rest of the 1990s continued. President Clinton was the first president "...whose administration has seen the shattering of more than one 1,000-point barrier. He is also the first Democrat to hold office when such a milestone was passed."[67]

As will be discussed in the section on Expansions of the Business Cycle (Section IV), some people think the 1990s stock market boom was due to the deficit reduction efforts of the Clinton White House. At the start of the Clinton administration, the US budget deficit was almost one trillion dollars. President Clinton and his staff proposed a four-year budget plan in 1993 that would cut that deficit in half. It was a combination of program reductions and tax increases that saved $500 billion in four years. This projected cut strengthened America's standing internationally, because it said that the US would do whatever it takes to get its financial house in order. The confidence it lent to investors in the stability and dependability of the payment of US debt allowed interest rates to remain low, due the very low risk of default.

With the passing of President Clinton's budget in 1993, the stock market was poised for a good run. Inflation was subdued, interest rates were relatively low, and the new budget projected a significant cut in the deficit. The timing of the business cycle was also favorable to growth in

President Clinton's first term. The economy was recovering from the recession of 1990–1991, and the stock market typically leads the recovery. Innovation is the key ingredient to any "prosperity" phase of the business cycle (see Section IV), and the 1990s boom was rich in technological innovation. The first web browser, Mosaic 1.0, became available in 1993, which made surfing the Internet a much easier thing to do. In March 1994, Apple released its first Macintosh computer with the PowerPC processor, which was a significant step forward in personal computer capability. In December 1994, Netscape released its first version of Netscape Navigator.[68]

By 1995, it was evident that something truly historic was happening in the US stock market. The Dow Jones Industrial Average (DJIA)had just passed 4,000 for the first time in February, and by the end of the year it would also pass the 5,000 milestone. In addition, in July 1995, the NASDAQ passed the 1,000 mark for the first time in its history. In March 1995, Yahoo! – the first web search service – was incorporated. The first Internet companies were getting noticed as "the next big thing," and the initial public offerings (IPOs) of these stocks were completely oversubscribed. Netscape, for example, doubled in price on its first day of trading, from the initial offering of $28 per share to $58.25, which gave it a market capitalization of $2.9 billion – not bad for a firm that was unprofitable.[69] In September 1995, eBay was founded.

IRRATIONAL EXUBERANCE IN THE STOCK MARKET

Then-Fed Chairman Alan Greenspan first used the phrase "irrational exuberance" to describe the behavior of stock market investors in December 1996.[70] In the prior month of November, following the 1996 presidential election, the Dow had 10 straight days of gains. At that point, the Dow had passed through the 6,000 mark and was well on its way (at almost 6,500) to passing the next 1,000-point barrier. Greenspan also noted that the stock market could have overpriced asset values. In July 1997, the Dow closed above 8,000, having doubled its value in two and a half years. In August of that year, Steve Jobs returned to Apple Computer, his NeXT company having been purchased by Apple nine months earlier.

Also in August 1997, Microsoft invested $150 million in Apple, and in return Apple received a guarantee from Microsoft that it would support Word and Excel for the Macintosh.[71]

In 1999, one of the largest Internet mergers ever occurred when Excite (an internet portal and web search engine) was purchased by @Home (a high-speed Internet cable service provider) for $6.7 billion. At its peak, the combined company had a stock price of over $120 per share and a market capitalization of over $35 billion. The purchase of GeoCities (a 3.5-million-subscriber Internet community) by Yahoo! (the internet search and web portal) for $4.6 billion in stock occurred soon thereafter, in January 1999.[72] At that time, the stock price of Yahoo! was $367 per share, and it was the darling of the stock market's dot-com era, peaking at over $800 per share (not split adjusted) in December 1999. However, since that time, the firm has seen its stock price fluctuate greatly, and it would never again capture those lofty heights. Excite @Home went bankrupt in 2001, when its stock price reached $1 per share and its assets were sold to pay off its debts.

THE Y2K EFFECT

Meanwhile, momentum was building for the event of the century – Y2K, or Year 2000. This event, and the worldwide concern it was generating from computer scientists, was starting to get national attention. The Y2K phenomenon was creating its own cottage industry. There were interest groups, associations, magazines, and societies dedicated to the eradication of potential software bugs that could cause computers to process data as if the date were January 1, 1900, instead of January 1, 2000. This industry maintained an almost religious zeal for making sure the world would be safe after midnight on December 31, 1999. As you can see in the numbers in Figure 10, the sales of computer equipment peaked in the last quarter of 1999, in line with completion of Y2K amelioration efforts.

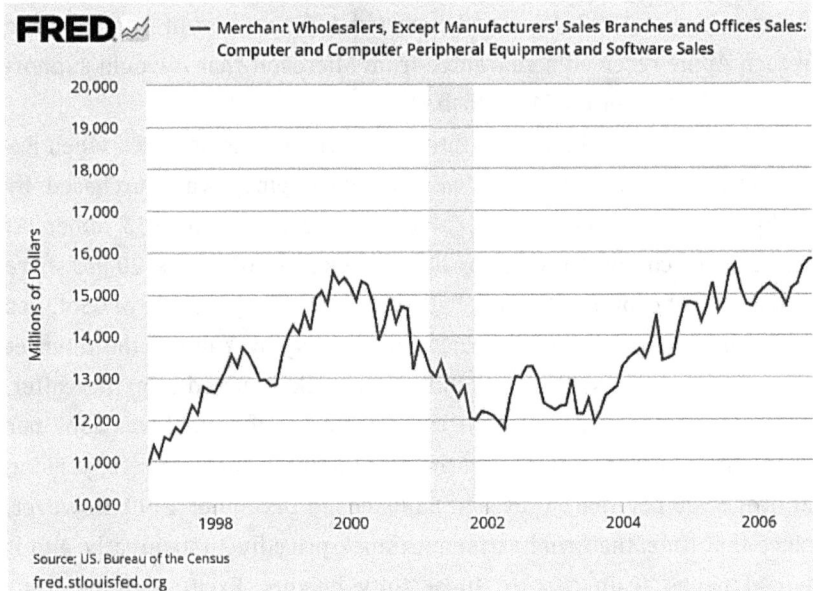

FRED — Merchant Wholesalers, Except Manufacturers' Sales Branches and Offices Sales: Computer and Computer Peripheral Equipment and Software Sales

Source: US. Bureau of the Census
fred.stlouisfed.org

Figure 10. Computer and Peripheral Equipment and Software Sales (1997-2007)[73]

The reason tech was so completely overriding everyone's concerns and expectations was Y2K. Remember that nonevent that occurred at the turn of the millennium? The reason why it was a nonevent was because of the billions upon billions of dollars being spent to make sure it was a nonevent. I was part of a Y2K team at Northrop Grumman when I was working on the Stealth Bomber. Every single computer on the airplane (and there were over 150 different computers processing close to two million source lines of software code) had to be validated. We had to guarantee that nothing would go wrong at the turn of the clock on January 1, 2000.

Every company and financial institution across the country and across the globe had similar Y2K teams working out their own analyses and validations of their hardware and software systems. The US financial system alone spent "many billions of dollars replacing and updating old systems and programs"[74] – and the Fed had crisis management teams in place in banks and districts around the country, with stockpiles of cash prepositioned in 90 locations. In addition, the Federal Open Market

Committee (FOMC) was prepared to release billions of dollars into the financial system to ensure its liquidity, in case there were any glitches. At the Fed's William McChesney Martin building in Washington, DC, they had installed extra televisions, phones, and computers to monitor the situation in real time, with over 100 people wearing "Federal Reserve Board Y2K Team" t-shirts.[75]

Similar situations played out across the country and around the world, with everyone on edge, because nobody knew exactly how well the issue had been mitigated or how other systems could impact their systems. The pressure was on, because no one wanted to be known as the company or system that led to the collapse of the global financial network or the demise of their industry. The stakes were high, and the problem was relatively well-defined: Any software or computer system in use had to be reviewed for Y2K rollover consequences and either modified, upgraded, or removed from the system and/or network. Every company, industry, and government agency had a team or organization assigned to Y2K in the US and globally. This was the state of affairs on December 31, 1999.

Well before that time, I was working on an MBA at the University of California in Irvine. I remember reading an article in *The Wall Street Journal* in 1998 about how much money was being spent on Y2K. Some time after reading that article, a classmate of mine asked me if I thought Y2K was going to be an issue. I told him that, with all the money being thrown at it, there was no way anyone was going to be caught unaware. I thought it was going to be a nonevent, and it was.

The easiest thing to do was to replace aging or older computers and software with newer computers and software that were already Y2K compliant. Who would want to take the risk of not finding that one line of code that could trip you up and kill your system, or have unidentifiable or undetermined behavior creep into your databases or information systems? Yes, the dot-com craze was a speculative time, but it was an augmentation on top of the very real and necessary growth of the computer industry to address the potential problem of Y2K.

THE Y2K BALLOON POPS

However, as soon as the crisis preparations had passed – as soon as the clock turned and the end of the world didn't happen – everything went back to normal. Normal, but with one very large exception: Nobody was buying computers. An entire industry saw a collapse in demand, due to the fact that several years' worth of computer replacements and upgrades had already been accomplished. It would be several years before the majority of the industry would recover and see demand for PCs and peripherals again. In addition, all those Y2K teams and consultants, an entire cottage industry of technical support, were no longer needed. Now those folks would be out of work, too.

As the need for computers, computer software, and technical support evaporated, it created a vacuum effect, sucking the air out of the stock/Internet/dot-com bubble. It also created a domino effect on the economy as a whole. As these high-paying tech jobs disappeared, so did the spending on toys, tools, and gadgets. As spending decreased, so did growth numbers across all industries. This, in turn, led not only to the stock market crash of 2000 but to the recession of 2001 as well. The collapse of the stock market also had a significant effect on tax revenue. Just as the federal budget was coming under control, due to the combination of taxes and spending cuts enacted by President Clinton, the next several years would see a significant decline in capital gains taxes. Unfortunately, at about this time, incoming-president George W. Bush based his tax cut on the premise of a large budget surplus that was being driven (at least partially) from revenue from stock capital gains taxes that would evaporate with the stock market crash.

It is interesting that the stock market peaked in March 2000. That makes sense to me, because the first quarter of the then-New Year after Y2K was going to have a sudden decrease in capital spending for computers and software. It affected a whole industry, as all the computer and software purchases had been completed prior to Y2K for the remaining next decade (or at least as long as computers usually last, which is about three years). Also, the cottage industry associated with fixing all those computer software programs, built in the 1960s through 1980s with a two-digit representation for the year, had all by then been fixed, so there was no longer any reason to retain those services.

THE 1929 DOW AND 2000 NASDAQ COMPARISON

The NASDAQ crash of 2000 is eerily similar to the crash of the Dow in 1929. If you adjust for time and amplitude (using a simple percentage formula), you can lay the two curves on top of each other and see that they follow the same pattern. The peak of the NASDAQ was 5,132.52 in March of 2000, and it took over 15 years to once again reach that mark. You can see in Figure 11 that the precipitous drop didn't all happen at once. There was the false rally in 2001. Then 9/11 occurred, and the bottom fell out. This is also what happened to the Dow after the crash of 1929. There was a short-lived "sucker's rally" in 1930. Then the bottom fell out. From there, it became a wave of panic, and selling was the name of the game. From October 1929 to the time the market hit bottom, about three years later, the Dow had lost almost 90% of its value. From March 2000 to the time the market hit bottom, about three years later, the NASDAQ had lost almost 80% of its value.

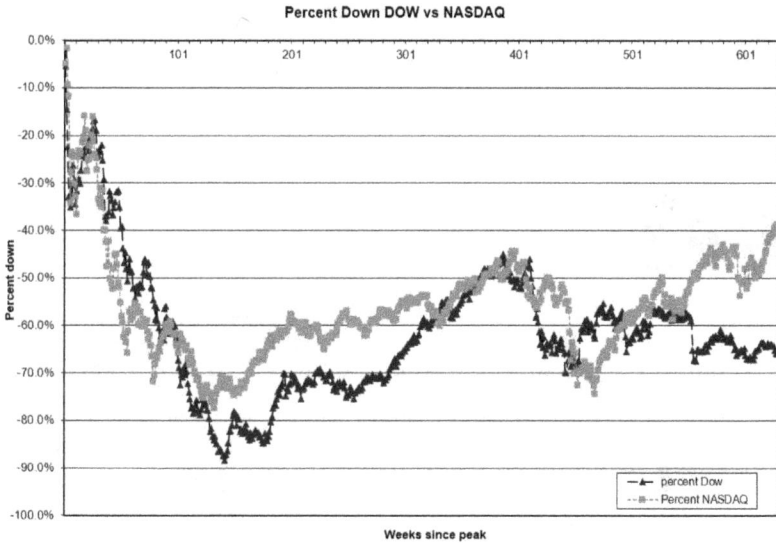

Figure 11. The 1929 Dow vs. The 2000 NASDAQ (Percentage)

I am not the only person who knows about the similarities between the 1929 Dow and the 2000 NASDAQ. In an article in *The Wall Street Journal*, titled "Eighty Years After the Great Crash – 'Is It the '30s Again?'" two authors, in light of the anniversary of the 1929 crash, discuss the question.[76] The interesting thing about this article is not the discussion but the inset graphic depicting the DJIA 1929–1939, NASDAQ 2000–2009, and DJIA 2007–2009. It was a percentage chart, similar to the chart above. The bottom line is, the curves replicate each other, and history repeats itself.

The comparisons don't end there. You can place the graph of the 1929 Dow on top of the 2000 NASDAQ and, adjusting for the time and scale factor, they line up right on top of each other, similar to Figure 11. As you can see in Figure 12, the parallels between the crash of 2000 and the crash of 1929 are astounding: the same initial decline (in a relative sense), the same sucker's rally, the same decline in the following years until year three. Some analysts predicted a turnaround in the stock market in 2003, and I believe that these analysts were following the same "predictor" that I show in Figure 12.

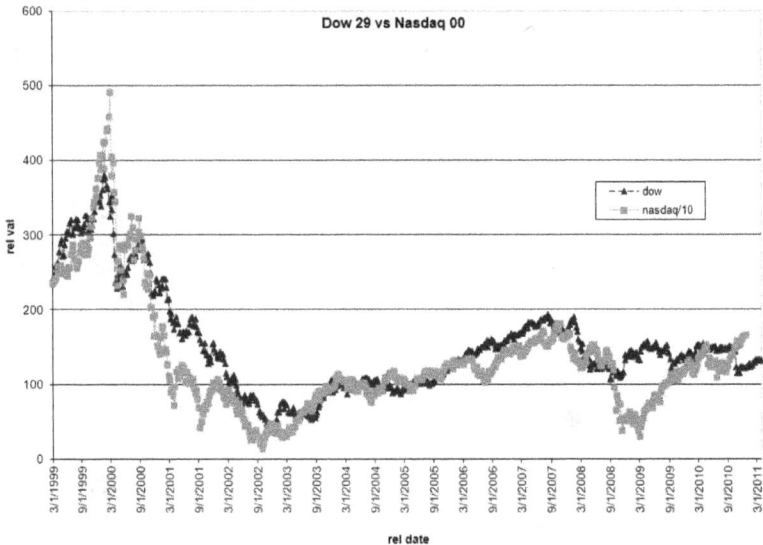

Figure 12. Stock Market "Predictor"

AN INVESTOR'S EDUCATION

I actually started my stock investing education at about this time. I took a course by Investools, which cost around $2,500. In this course, I learned about momentum investing, 200-day moving averages, stochastics, oversold, overbought, and many other technical terms in the investing field. I consider this one of the most valuable courses I have ever had. What better way to spend your money and time than to learn how to make money?

As I tested the limits of my education in this area, I learned many lessons. The market is a strict teacher. I used the money I had in my 401k (rolled over into a Charles Schwab IRA) to fund my education in the stock market. That is, my investment lessons were learned using my own retirement account. This was not my brightest idea, because it was quite a risk to gamble with my retirement savings. But as a financially struggling parent and husband, it was the only money I had to work with.

In 2003, there were many opportunities to make money in the market. Some stocks, like TASR, were on a meteoric rise. The company Taser, which makes the electronic stun-gun used by many police departments across the country, was on a tear. I wanted to buy in, but the stock price just kept rising. Then one day, it dropped, for some unexplained reason. Here was my chance, and I took it. Unfortunately, this was my first lesson in how the market punishes bad news. I lost a lot of money on that stock. I didn't have any rules on how to limit my losses, and I held that stock for far too long, losing over 50% of my investment. Now when I hear the phrase "never try to catch a falling knife," I know what it means. I have learned well that harsh lesson.

A second lesson on how the market punishes bad news was my investment in Krispy Kreme Doughnuts (symbol: KKD). Krispy Kreme was a Philadelphia-based corporation that had expanded to the West, and it was a local hit in southern California. As they say in stock market investing, invest in what you know and what you like. I loved Krispy Kreme doughnuts, and when one opened in a nearby mall, I stood in line to be one of the first to try them. I enjoyed it so much, I took the plunge and purchased the stock.

It wasn't long after I invested in this stock that *The Wall Street Journal* published an article on KKD's overexpansion and potential earnings issues.[77] The story was, they had bought back several franchises and then used the purchases to boost earnings, even though this should have been shown as a loss. There were even hints or allegations of earnings manipulation and a potential SEC investigation. The stock plunged on the news. I couldn't get out of that stock fast enough. And as a full-time employee, I couldn't sell the stock while at work on company time, so I wasn't able to sell until the next day.

I took a bath on both of these examples. With these lessons (and some others I will not bother to mention), I have decided that individual stocks don't work for me. I am more easily able to watch the overall market than keep up with individual stocks. For these reasons, I now almost exclusively purchase exchange-traded funds (ETFs). ETFs are a basket of stocks that are managed by a firm to represent an index, or possibly a leveraged basket of funds to emulate the inverse, or multiple, of an index.

Because I follow the overall market and understand the correlation between the economy and how the market reacts to the general health of the economy, I am better able to invest in market indexes than individual stocks. In addition, by using my experience with cycles and trends, I am better able to forecast where I think the market is headed. Finally, investing in indexes provides more liquidity with less cost (in terms of fees) than mutual funds or individual stocks. Remember: You can make money in any market (up, down, or sideways), as long as you know where it is headed.

Just because I don't invest in individual stocks doesn't mean you shouldn't. I am only saying that I have not had much success in that arena. If you do decide to invest in individual stocks, I would recommend that you read *Rule #1* by Phil Town. In my stock market investing education, I have read all the classics – *The Intelligent Investor* by Benjamin Graham, *Common Stocks and Uncommon Profits* by Philip Fisher, *One Up on Wall Street* by Peter Lynch, *How to Make Money in Stocks* by William O'Neal, *Beating the Dow with Bonds* by Michael O'Higgins, and many others. In my opinion, you only need to read one book – Phil Town's. His work distills the essence of most of these other books into a clear and easy-to-understand approach to stock market investing. Rule #1 is: Don't lose money.

Chapter 6.
The Great Crash of 1929

The 1929 stock market crash and its subsequent downward spiral were the worst in history and the start of the Great Depression. The Dow Jones Industrial Average eventually lost almost 90% of its peak value. When US leaders reacted to that crisis, they did exactly the opposite of what they should have done. They should have flooded the system with easy money and guaranteed the deposits of banks, but instead they let banks fail. They should have provided a stimulus, but instead they tightened credit and increased interest rates. The result of these policies was a liquidity crunch that seized up the economy, as companies found themselves unable to finance continued operations. Modern-day economists and federal regulators are biased by this history and viewpoint; as a result, they view every stock market crash or down cycle as having the potential to cause the next Great Depression.[78]

American debt and banking failures were among the causes of the prolonged slump after the 1929 crash. Accumulated debt by businesses and households, due to the excesses of the 1920s cheap-money policies and leveraging to take advantage of stock market opportunities, took some time to untangle. The deleveraging process lasted many years, as falling prices and increases in unemployment made the repayment of debt more difficult and extended the process. "In particular, it set into motion a vicious spiral within which everybody's efforts to reduce that load for a time only availed to increase it."[79]

After the 1929 stock market crash, most business forecasts expected a recession and a general downturn of the economy in 1930. What they saw that year was a tale of two halves (but it would turn out to be "the haves and the have-nots"). The first half of 1930 saw a stock market rally, as the Dow improved from a low of 248 at the beginning of the year to a high of 294 in April. The second half of the year saw the Dow fall steadily, as liquidations occurred in multiple rounds and the contraction quickened; "...people felt that the ground under their feet was giving way."[80] The Dow ended at 170 by the end of the year.

If 1930 was an unsettling contradiction, then 1931 was outright panic. The Dow plunged from a high of 190 in February to less than 80 by the end of the year. Physical production continued to contract through 1931 and into 1932. Price levels fell throughout that period and so did the cost of living. Agricultural prices tumbled about 65% from 1929 to the end of 1932. Demand deposits at federal banks held firm through the middle of 1931 but then declined sharply through May 1932. Industrial payrolls dropped to about 40% of their 1925 averages by the middle of 1932. Hourly wages also fell through the middle of 1933.[81]

The Dow bottomed out in July 1932 at 41, almost 90% below its peak of 380 in 1929. The stock market rallied up to 76 in September and then fell again back down to 60 by the end of the 1932 election year. Then, New York Governor Franklin Roosevelt defeated President Hoover by a landslide in the November election, and the country eagerly awaited his inauguration. However, at that time, the presidential inauguration wasn't held until March of the year following an election. Because of the dire economic consequences and the time criticality of the situation, Congress enacted the 20th Amendment to the Constitution (ratified in 1933), which moved up presidential inaugurations from March 4 to January 20. This was also known as the "Lame Duck" amendment, but it didn't become effective until President Roosevelt's second term.

A NEW PRESIDENT AND A NEW THEORY

Once President Roosevelt took office in March, the stock market improved and went from 55 to over 100 by July. One of the first actions the president implemented was a bank holiday – he closed all the banks in the United States to give them time to respond to the banking crisis. There were runs on banks throughout the nation, and the president believed they were caused by people panicking and losing confidence in the system. He began his "fireside chats" on the radio on March 12. As the decade of the 1930s rolled on, the depression worsened, but eventually the combined effects of the New Deal programs and the implementation of economic theories espoused by economist John Maynard Keynes put an end to the Depression by the end of the decade.

John Maynard Keynes was a British economist whose theories on macroeconomics became the basis for how the Roosevelt administration would fight the Great Depression. Basically, Keynes believed that only strong government intervention could reduce or avert the unemployment and economic malaise caused by the business cycle. He especially attacked the neoclassical economists who believed in laissez-faire policies. Upon the publication of his book, *The General Theory of Employment, Interest, and Money*, his theories were termed "Keynesian economics." With the successful implementation of the New Deal and the positive impacts these government policies had in reducing unemployment and increasing fiscal stability, Keynes became regarded as a modern-day Adam Smith. The well-known economist Milton Friedman was once quoted as saying, "We're all Keynesians now."

The essence of what Keynes proposed was that government could and should take part in managing the economy. It is difficult to compare what is widely accepted today as economic fact with the abiding theories and assumptions of the day back in the 1930s. What Keynes was espousing back at that time was somewhat revolutionary – government was not expected nor welcomed to take a part in the control of the economy. Per Adam Smith's doctrine, the "invisible hand" of supply and demand controlled the economy. The classical economists believed that wages and prices would automatically rise and fall, depending on the basic factors existing in the general economy. What Keynes proposed was that employment could get "stuck" at a level reflecting what reasonable people thought were expected wages. Specifically, he stated: "...workers will not seek a much greater money-wage when employment improves or allow a very great reduction rather than suffer any unemployment at all."[82]

MISHANDLING OF A CRISIS

Economist John Kenneth Galbraith stated that a balanced budget and the maintenance of the gold standard (fear of inflation) were the economic principles of the day. He called this the "...triumph of dogma over thought."[83] The economic advisors to President Hoover, including Treasury Secretary Mellon and Federal Reserve Chairman Young, urged restraint and caution in dealing with the crisis. President Hoover himself wrote a message to President-elect Roosevelt to maintain adherence to the balanced budget. Galbraith was a Keynesian, who thought that monetarism was "... a feeble reed on which to lean."[84] But he also stated that the government's lack of response to the stock market crash affected the breadth and depth of the resulting depression: "The rejection of fiscal (tax and expenditure) and monetary policy amounted precisely to a rejection of all affirmative government economic policy."[85]

Because of the relatively small US middle-income population in the 1920s and 1930s, the impact of the stock market crash on the wealthy had a disproportionately large effect on consumer spending, savings, and investment, and that affected the overall economy. Holding companies and investment trusts, two relatively new financial constructs in the 1920s, were partially responsible for the significant stock market decline in the 1930s. Financial institutions of the time were unable to effectively deal with their collapse. Just as we dealt with how to deleverage and untangle from the credit default swaps and collateralized debt obligations (CDOs) of the 2008 real estate collapse, the financial institutions of the 1930s were dealing with how to untangle from the investment trusts and holding companies of that era.

TECHNOLOGY DRIVEN INNOVATION AND SPECULATION

Like the Y2K NASDAQ, the 1929 Dow was driven by new technologies and exploitation of those technologies. In 1929, it was the automobile and the automotive industry (General Motors, Ford), airplanes and aviation (Wright Aeronautic), and electronics and radio (General Electric, RCA). In 2000, it was the semiconductor transistor (Intel), which led to computers (Dell, Apple) and the information technology industry, including the Internet (Yahoo, Netscape). This technology-driven cycle of creation, innovation, acceptance, and exploitation explains the cyclical nature of the stock market long cycle. I relate these to the long-term Kondratieff cycle, at least in terms of the industry drivers (new product innovation) and their effects.

As with all speculative fevers, the run-ups don't all happen at once. In 1928, the year before the Great Crash, Wright Aeronautic soared from 69 to 289, Radio Corporation of America (RCA) amped up to 420 from 85, and Montgomery Ward almost quadrupled to 440 from 117.[86] Aiding the speculative fervor was the publicity surrounding these events. Newspapers regularly quoted business leaders pontificating about the new order of things and the rosy outlook. The press also included human-interest stories about people who got rich from one stock or another. This led to the mass-market psychology and frenzy associated with the run-up.

Prior to the Y2K crash, pundits were saying how the Internet made everything different and that the old rules didn't apply – company valuations of astronomical earnings per share (EPS) were purported to be valid, even if the company had yet to make a profit.

HISTORY REPEATS ITSELF

Some people have used the post-1929 Dow graph (adjusted for time and scale factors) as a predictor for how the NASDAQ will behave (see Figure 12). Over time, it has been a fairly decent forecaster of the general direction of the market, and it can be used (potentially) to show the overall trend. In fact, I used the predictor to convince myself that there would be a stock market crash in 2008. I used that, in combination with knowledge of a tax-law change in 2008 that allowed for zero taxes on long-term capital gains for persons within a certain income bracket, and the expectation that there would be a recession in 2009 (the stock market leads the business cycle by six months, so I expected a downturn in the stock market in 2008, due to the coming recession).

I used my expectation of a stock market crash in 2008 to short the market and double my money in one year. In January 2008, I shorted the

NASDAQ QQQ (also known as "the Qs"). When the stock market crashed in October of 2008, I managed to double my money that year.

I also used the Dow-NASDAQ predictor to double my money the next year. My expectation was that stocks would bounce back, so I purchased an ETF that would perform twice what the QQQ did. I purchased the stock for just over $30 per share, and by the end of 2009, it had also doubled to over $60 per share. In addition, they kept rising, so I held on-to my stock as it went beyond $90 for a 200% return on my investment. Then, as the old saying goes, "pigs get fat, hogs get slaughtered" – I held onto the stock, hoping it would get to $120 per share. The US and European debt crisis of 2011 taught me a valuable lesson in humility.

THE LESSONS OF HISTORY

If there are such similarities between the 1929 crash and the stock market crash of 2000, then why wasn't there a great depression at the turn of this century? The answer to that question is that we learned from history. The 1929 stock market crash is one of the most studied events in US history. In fact, former Fed Chairman Ben Bernanke did his PhD dissertation on that event. What we learned from the 1929 crash was that in the early 1900s, economics was not a very well-developed field of study. As a result of the crisis, economists from all over the world took a new look at the causes and potential mitigating actions that could minimize the risk of future dire scenarios. The works of Keynes, Fisher, Schumpeter, Friedman, and many other economists have vastly improved our understanding of macroeconomic events and consequences.

One of the best things President George W. Bush did was to propose a significant tax cut in 2001 after the stock market crash of 2000. This tax cut put thousands of dollars back in the hands of consumers. It took the budget surplus of the 1990s (and projected tax revenues in future years) and put it back in the hands of consumers (and taxpayers). The law provided tax cuts for all income earners and limited the highest end tax bracket to 33%. It also lowered the estate tax and raised the allowable no-tax inheritance to $1 million. His proposed tax cut would cost $1.6 trillion over 10 years, or about $160 billion per year. This government stimulus was a great boost to the economy and did a lot to ensure a quick recovery from the twin economic shocks of the 2000 stock market crash and the terrorist attacks on 9/11.[87]

Whereas it took an extremely long time for the economy and financial institutions to deal with the fallout of the 1929 stock market crash, it only took a couple of years for the economy and financial institutions to recover from the 2008 real estate collapse. I believe this is due to how Fed Chairman Ben Bernanke and Treasury Secretary Hank Paulson handled the crisis: They immediately and overwhelmingly provided liquidity to the market. That continued into 2014, with the quantitative easing that remained in effect until October of that year, which bought billions of dollars in Treasuries and mortgage-backed securities. I think we can especially credit Bernanke with providing the steady hand that righted the ship as the economy navigated a sea of danger and potential doom. The actions of Bernanke and the Fed contributed to a quick recovery of the stock market to its present performance (all-time highs for the Dow and the S&P).

There is another stock market cyclical effect that is described in the following section. This is known as the "channeling" effect, and it has to do with the market going sideways for an extended period of time. If you spot this trend, you can also make money, but you have to know when it is in effect and how long you can expect it to last. When the market is under this condition, it is no time to "buy and hold" – because your stock will go up and down and likely end up where it started. I call this the secular bear market – secular because it lasts a long time. There is also the secular bull market, which is the long-run bull market; I call these combined secular effects the 36-year Stock Super Cycle.

Chapter 7.
The Stock Super Cycle

The very first stock cycle started about 100 years ago, when the Dow index on the New York Stock Exchange was first established. To understand the cycle, here's a brief history: The Dow and the New York Stock Exchange are inextricably linked. The seminal event that created the NYSE was the signing of the Buttonwood Agreement on May 17, 1792. Under a buttonwood tree on Wall Street is where twenty-four stockbrokers met to sign the document that defined their rules for buying and selling shares. On March 8, 1817, these brokers drafted a constitution and called themselves the New York Stock & Exchange Board.[88] For the first 100 years of the NYSE, the only way you could be informed about stock prices was to be a member of the exchange. That all changed with the creation of *The Wall Street Journal* and the Dow.

Charles Dow, Edward Jones, and Charles Bergstresser founded Dow, Jones & Company in 1882.[89] The Dow Jones Industrial Average was created by Charles Dow and was intended to provide an estimate of the relative health and activity of the stocks traded on the NYSE. Dow Jones & Company also planned to create a newspaper and a newswire to provide full coverage of the financial market. With the Dow Jones index's official launch in 1896, combined with the advent of *The Wall Street Journal* in 1889, financial journalism provided a way of communicating information about the stocks and bonds traded on the NYSE and an overall indication of the health of Wall Street.

Charles Dow chose twelve companies as the original list for his index: the American Cotton Oil Company; American Sugar Company; American Tobacco Company; Chicago Gas Company; Distilling & Cattle Feeding

Company; Edison General Electric Company; Laclede Gas Company; National Lead Company; North American Company; Tennessee Coal, Iron and Railroad Company; US Leather Company; and United States Rubber Company. This index grew to fourteen companies and then to thirty companies, which is the number the Dow includes today. The list of companies that make up the index has changed over the years, as technology and the market have evolved, but the index has remained at thirty companies since it was revised to that number in 1928.[90]

THE FIRST SUPER CYCLE

The early years of the NYSE and the DJIA were marked by several financial "panics" – including the Panic of 1901, the Panic of 1907, and the Panic of 1910–1911. These panics were usually associated with liquidity issues and bank runs, which would cause a domino effect as bank loans were recalled to provide the needed cash to hold off a bank run, which would fail and cause businesses to default. In order to deal with these liquidity issues in the future, Congress created the Federal Reserve System.[91]

With the creation of the Federal Reserve, financial stability provided the foundation upon which the first up cycle of the stock market occurred. From a low of 52 in 1914 to a market peak of 351 in 1929, the stock market boomed. It was the Roaring '20s, and anything was possible. In fact, John Raskob, the former president of General Motors and future financier of the Empire State Building, said as much in an interview for the *Ladies' Home Journal* in August 1929, titled "Everybody Ought to Be Rich." It seemed as if everyone was investing in the stock market, and most people were buying on margin. As is the case with any speculative bubble, all good things must come to an end, and that occurred on Black Thursday, October 24, 1929.

That was the first stock market cycle – the secular bear market from 1896 (when the Dow was at 41) to 1914 (the Dow at 52), and then the secular bull market from 1914 to 1929 (the Dow at 351). This pattern has repeated in an overall cycle of 36 years as the stock super cycle (a combination of the 18-year secular bear cycle and the 18-year secular bull cycle) for the past 100 years. I recognize that the initial pattern was 18 years for the bear cycle and only 15 years for the bull. However, the averages of these super cycles are 17.3 years for the secular bear market and 17.6 years for the secular bull market.

THE SECOND SUPER CYCLE

The second cycle started with the next bear market from 1930 (the Dow at 162) to 1945 (the Dow at 190). These years were especially harsh for the stock market and the general economy. The Great Depression was a hardship for so many people, as unemployment soared and banks failed. The Dow went from 351 in 1929 to as low as 41 in 1932. The Securities Act of 1933 provided transparency and disclosure rules for the stock market, and The Securities Exchange Act of 1934 added regulations so that unscrupulous executives who manipulated their company's public information would face criminal prosecution.[92] The stock market sank again in 1937, as the Dow dropped over 100 points. World War II started in 1939, when Germany invaded Poland. And in 1941, the US entered the war after Japan attacked Pearl Harbor. This left the market struggling, as the Dow dipped below 120; however, the US economy put men and women to work building airplanes, tanks, guns, and bombs to fight the war, and the stock market recovered.

The next up cycle occurred after WWII ended and as our service men and women came home. The Dow was at 180 in 1946 and hit 900 in 1965. The US population exploded with the return of all those soldiers to start families and return to their lives. It was the start of the baby boom generation, and its demographic drove the market for much of the rest of the century. In 1948, President Harry S. Truman was re-elected, to the surprise of many in the media, defeating the expected winner Thomas E. Dewey. The Korean War started in 1950, as a Chinese-equipped North Korean army swarmed a lightly armed UN force. This was the official start of the Cold War. After the cease-fire in 1953 and an end to the hostilities, the Dow renewed its upward trend.

The Dow jumped from 290 in 1953 to over 400 in 1954. General Dwight D. Eisenhower was elected president in 1952 and re-elected in

1956, when the market hit 500. During his eight years as president, the Dow rose over 100%. Then the Sputnik satellite was launched in 1957, and that put a damper on things, as people then worried about the "technology gap" between the US and the USSR. But the market eventually recovered and passed 600 in February of 1959. As President Kennedy took office in 1961 (having beaten Richard Nixon in a heavily contested election in 1960), the stock market continued its run and passed the 700 mark in May. The Cuban Missile Crisis shook investor confidence in 1962, and the Dow dropped down to the mid-500s. However, after nuclear war was averted, the market climbed back through 700 and was in the mid-700s by the end of 1963. The market passed through 800 in February of 1964 and peaked at 900 in January 1965.

THE THIRD SUPER CYCLE

The third stock market super cycle started in 1965 and went through 1982 for the bear portion of the cycle (17 years). From that market peak of 900 in early 1965, it was another seven years before it reached that level again. Many factors weighed on the market. Inflation was a constant battle, from the administrations of Presidents Johnson and Nixon through those of Presidents Ford and Carter; inflation was a drain on the economy and a drag on the market. The Vietnam War raged abroad, and civil unrest and turmoil erupted domestically.

In January 1968, the Tet (New Year) Offensive started in Vietnam, which surprised the US with its fierceness and caused the American government to rethink its role in the region. Shortly thereafter, President Johnson declared he would not seek re-election. In April 1968, Dr. Martin Luther King Jr. was assassinated, and race riots occurred throughout the country. While on the campaign trail in Indianapolis, Bobby Kennedy spoke to a group gathered for a rally and told them all that Dr. King had been killed. He related that he understood how they all felt, because someone close to him had been killed (he was speaking about his brother, President John Kennedy). That was the only major city in the country that didn't have riots. Two months later, Bobby Kennedy was assassinated while campaigning for the Democratic nomination in California. In

November, Richard Nixon was elected president of the United States, and the market ended a down year near 820.

In 1969, the Dow dropped again, to a number slightly over 700. It was a year of many challenges and some successes – there were many protests of the Vietnam War and demonstrations in Chicago, but it was also the year Neil Armstrong walked on the moon. Finally, the market started to rebound, and by 1970 it was back over 800 again. The year 1971 was relatively flat for the Dow, but 1972 saw it rise to new heights. The Dow officially broke the 1,000 barrier on November 14, 1972. It was a brief passage through that milestone, as several significant events were on the horizon. President Nixon had won a landslide victory in the November election; however, details of the Watergate break-in and subsequent cover-up would hit the headlines in 1973. In addition, in the other major event of 1973, the OPEC oil embargo would wreak havoc on the economy and the stock market. The economy saw a major recession in 1973 and a bear market in 1973–1974. The Dow dipped as low as 577 in December 1974.

The stock market recovered much of its earlier losses from the recession and the '73–'74 bear market in 1975, and by 1976 the Dow was back up to 1,000. The economy was doing better, and President Ford was actually making some progress fighting the war on inflation. However, in the presidential election of 1976, the American people decided they didn't want to re-elect a president they had never elected in the first place, and the Democrat from Georgia, James Earl Carter, was elected president. Whether it was his response to the Soviet invasion of Afghanistan, his inability to control inflation, the unemployment rate, stagflation, or his response to the Iranian hostage crisis, the Carter presidency was not kind to the stock market. During President Carter's term in office, the Dow went from 1,000 to as low as 750.

The stock market eventually rebounded and climbed back up to respectably, ending 1980 above 960. The election of 1980 swept former California Governor Ronald Reagan into the White House. Inflation gripped the economy and unemployment was still running high, but the Iranian hostages were freed on the day of Reagan's inauguration. President Reagan also survived an assassination attempt early in the first year of his presidency. He worked with Fed Chairman Paul Volcker to enact a plan to wring inflation out of the economy. Chairman Volcker tightened the money supply and strangled inflation by squeezing excess funds out of the system. This caused a severe recession in 1981–1982, but the US economy came out of it stronger than ever before. This strangling of inflation cured the economy and set up the stock market for its greatest growth period in history – the up phase of the third cycle of the stock market, with the Dow skyrocketing from 1,000 to 10,000.

THE STOCK MARKET BOOM

From mid-1982 to early 2000 (about 18 years), the stock market and the Dow rose to unprecedented and unexpected levels. The passing of the Dow through each thousand-level milestone brought celebrations and elation on Wall Street and on Main Street. There were a few bumps on the road, most notably the crash of 1987, but on the whole and looking back in retrospect, it was a grand time to be an investor. From a low of 776 in 1982, the Dow climbed to 2,000 in less than five years. President Reagan may have provided the impetus for this bull run. His "supply-side" economics provided a tax cut of $750 million, and he drastically increased defense spending. With inflation fading and unemployment stabilizing, the economy improved.

In 1984, President Reagan won re-election for his second term in office by the largest-ever difference in the electoral vote (525 to 13). In 1985, President Reagan and Soviet President Mikhail Gorbachev held a summit meeting in Geneva, Switzerland. They found common ground and created a bond that would have implications later on. The Dow hit 1,500 in December of 1985 and then passed through 2,000 a little more than a year later. In August 1987, the Dow peaked at 2,722, and two months later, it had one of the largest one-day declines in stock market history. The Dow dropped over 500 points on October 19, 1987, which was on par, percentage-wise, with the Dow drop in the 1929 stock market crash. I still remember that day and the feeling of panic and fear that gripped the people I worked with. They were mostly older than me, 50 or 60 years old, and they were seeing their retirement accounts devastated by this one-day drop. At the time, I was in my 20s, so it didn't have the same impact on me.

The market didn't stay down for long. Alan Greenspan, the new Fed chairman, opened up the money supply to keep liquidity in the market. In addition, President Reagan didn't comment on the crash, which some say may have had a more calming effect than if he had gone on television to reassure the public.[93] The Dow was back over 2,000 by the end of 1987 and passed the 2,722 mark (its last peak) in 1989. George H. W. Bush was elected president in 1988 and was inaugurated in January 1989. On November 9, 1989, the Berlin wall came down, and that brought about significant political and economic changes in Europe. By 1990, the Dow flirted with 3,000, coming just shy of the mark at 2,999 in July. Then in August, Saddam Hussein's forces in Iraq invaded Kuwait, and the stock market slid down to 2,365 by October.

President Bush, backed by international condemnation of Hussein's actions, gathered a coalition of forces to oust Hussein from Kuwait. January 16, 1991, was an unforgettable date in history, as it was the day Operation Desert Storm and the Iraq war started. Operation Desert Storm was over quickly, as the American Coalition forces routed the Iraqi army and Red Guard. It was an overwhelming victory for the allies, and the stock market also won. By April, the Dow was over 3,000. The quick victory in Iraq, combined with the end of the Cold War (the effects of the demolition of the Berlin Wall and of free elections in former Eastern European Soviet states), started a significant reduction in US defense spending and coincided with a recession in 1991. The effects of this recession, an increase in unemployment, and a weakened economy in 1992 made re-election chances slim for President Bush. He was disappointed in the lack of support he received from the Fed in addressing the sluggish economy, and he went as far as to say Alan Greenspan was the cause of the country's economic woes. In November 1992, Bill Clinton won the election for president with the slogan, "It's the economy, stupid."[94]

President Clinton presided over the most remarkable run of successive Dow milestones in history. In the eight years he was president, from

January 1993 through the year 2000, the Dow broke seven 1,000-mark milestones. It broke 4,000 in February 1995 and from there soared – at times, seemingly inexorably – to 10,000 in March 1999. As impressive a climb and bull market as this was, it wasn't smooth sailing the entire period. In October 1997, the Dow dropped 554 points in one day, similar to the drop in October 1987. However, this fall wasn't as dramatic, because it wasn't as significant in percentage terms. The 508-point drop on October 19, 1987, was almost a 23% decline in one day. The 554-point drop on October 27, 1997, was only a 7% decline of a 7,900-level Dow. In addition, the "circuit breakers" put in place after the 1987 experience successfully kept the Dow from tumbling further.[95] The circuit breakers were implemented to stop computerized trading when certain market conditions exist.

THE FOURTH SUPER CYCLE

President Bill Clinton's last year running the country and overseeing the economy and the stock market wasn't as successful as his first seven years. The Dow peaked at 11,722 on January 14, 2000, and it didn't see that level again for almost seven years. The Dow fell to as low as 7,286 on October 9, 2002. The Dow dropped, but not as much as the tech-laden NASDAQ did. As I've already explained, the NASDAQ fell by the same percentage as the Dow in the Crash of 1929. And just as it was in that prior cycle, it started the cyclical bear phase of the next stock market super cycle. Exactly five years to the day after the Dow's low in 2002, on October 9, 2007, it peaked at 14,164. Then in 2008, the financial crisis occurred, and the Dow plummeted again. It sank to a low of 6,547 on March 9, 2009. This reflects the cyclical bear phase of the stock market super cycle, as the Dow vacillates above and below the 10,000 level.

The stock market has multiple cycles operating simultaneously. It is extremely sensitive to the 9-year business cycle, and is affected by the expansion-recession periods of that cycle. The stock market is also affected by an overall "secular" cycle. The overall cycle has a length of 36 years and two components: an 18-year period of flat or level (secular bear) performance, and an 18-year period of steadily increasing (secular bull) performance that reaches the next "level" value. These periods are easily seen on a graph of the DJIA on semi-logarithmic paper and are called Stock Super Cycles (Figure 13). There have been three of these cycles in the last 100 years.

Dow Jones Industrial Average

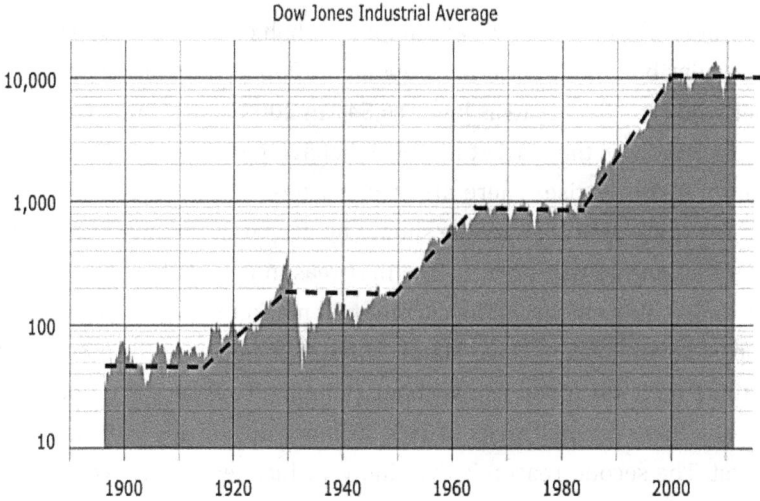

Figure 13. The Stock Super Cycle

- Cycle 1: The first stock market cycle started with the secular bear market from 1896 (when the Dow was at 41) to 1914 (the Dow at 52). Then the first secular bull market occurred, and during the Roaring '20s, the Dow climbed from a low of 63 to a peak of 371 in 1929.
- Cycle 2: The second stock market cycle started with the Crash of 1929, and the Dow and the country went through a depression that lasted until World War II. From 1946 to 1965, the Dow went from 200 to 1,000. That was the period of the "Nifty 50" stocks – so called because, no matter what the price of one of those shares was when you purchased it, it just kept going up.

- Cycle 3: From 1965 to 1982, the Dow hovered around 1,000 for 17 years. It was a period of war, civil unrest, inflation, and stagflation. Then the Dow went from 1,000 in 1982 to 10,000 in 2000. That 18-year period was the most expansive and profitable on record.

I would postulate that we are in the first half of the fourth super cycle, the secular bear half. Since the Dow hit 10,000 in 2000, it has been another wild ride. It sunk to as low as 6,547 in 2009 and in 2017 went over 21,000. Recently, the market has been behaving nicely, and the Dow has been on a steady rise. There are two reasons why I feel this is a risky time for stocks and that people should be prepared to jump out of equities if the market turns south. The first reason is that there is a limit to how long a bull run lasts. The current bull market has been going on for the past several years, since March 2009. It is very rare for a market to continue on a sustained run without some pullback at some point, and typically there are pullbacks of 10% or more during any bull run of the market. The second reason is the nine-year business cycle: We are eight years into that cycle (as of 2017), and as they say – all good things must come to an end. This will be discussed more thoroughly in the next chapter.

Chapter 8.
What's Next for the Stock Market

Typically, money moves to the site of highest returns. Currently, there seem to be no alternatives for good returns on investment than the stock market. However, that will change at some point in the future. The question is, when? As I look at the current chart of the DJIA at over 20,000 (in 2017), I wonder how long this current run will last. Most bull markets or bear markets last from two to five years. This current bull market is more than eight years old, so it should be coming to an end. Or will it?

To answer that question, you need to consider the business cycle and relate that to how and when you should make investment decisions. The current business cycle, which will be discussed in detail in Section IV, is eight years into a nine-year cycle (as of 2017). Since the last recession occurred in 2009, I would expect the next recession by 2018 and, since the stock market leads the economy by about six months, I would expect a bear market by the end of 2017 or beginning of 2018.

A similar correlation to return on investment could be made to current real estate trends. The real estate market has bottomed out and has seen some areas regain some of their earlier losses. This is not true of all regions (remember that real estate is a locally driven phenomenon – "location, location, location"), as some areas are still well below their 2006 peak. What would happen if there were a major stock market correction in 2017? It could spark a significant shift in investments back into real estate (inflation will also cause this).

We had seen prior Dow high points (before the Great Recession) of almost 14,000 in June of 2007, and as the Dow rises above 20,000 in

2017, it makes you wonder how high it can go. However, it is very risky at these higher levels and difficult to predict when the peak will be. So, it would be wise to watch very carefully how the market is responding to economic and political conditions. Remember: When it comes to the stock market, bad things usually happen in October.

THE NEXT BEAR MARKET

In the short term (the next couple years), I don't expect the stock market to be the best place to put your cash, only because I believe in the channeling theory that states the market will be suffering from a secular bear run from 2000 to 2018, with an average value of 10,000. During this time period, it would be unwise to adopt a buy-and-hold approach as your investment strategy. The best tactic would be to buy at the dips and sell at the tops. In essence, this is what is called "timing the market" – which everyone will tell you is difficult to do. I agree that it is difficult; however, it would be well worth the trouble. In a declining market, it is better to take control of your portfolio and manage it through those troubled waters than to watch with fear and trepidation as someone else sails your savings lifeboat into the rocky shore.

The Dow hit 10,000 (adjusted close) on March 29, 1999. What this tells us is that the current stock market will stay relatively flat until about 2018. People who are in those "cycle funds" are in for a rude awakening. If they started in 2000 and have a 2020 fund, they will find out that, after 18 years of "aggressive" risk taking in the stock market, they will see their portfolio turn to "safe" investments in bonds, just as the market will be taking off in the next great bull run of the 2020s.

You may ask, "Well, how do I know how to time the dips and the tops?" The answer is, "pay attention." In the secular bear market for this particular Super Cycle, the market will channel along an area within a few thousand points of 10,000. When the Dow goes higher than 10,000 points, the market will pull back toward the mean, sooner or later. The opposite is also true – when the Dow goes lower than 10,000 points, the market will push it back up to the mean. The net effect is to keep the Dow average floating at about 10,000. So, when the Dow is much greater than 10,000, you should consider that an overbought market and pay close attention to the opportunities to sell. When the Dow is in a bear market and goes much lower than 10,000, you should consider that an oversold market and look for opportunities to buy. Please note that "much greater" and "much lower" are relative to a semi-logarithmic scale, which would be several thousand points above or below 10,000.

What's next for the stock market will depend on the year in question. You need to know where you are in the cycle to show the expected return. I believe we are in a dangerous time for stocks right now, as the market is above 20,000. We also need to consider the business cycle, and relate that to how we make investment decisions. The current business cycle, which will be discussed in detail in the next section, is eight years into a nine-year cycle (as of 2017). The peak of the business cycle occurred in 2014, or early 2015, even though it didn't feel as it were peaking. Then a gradual slowdown should be expected by no later than early 2017. I would expect the next major recession to occur by 2018, and since the stock market leads the economy by about six months, I would expect a bear market to start by the end of 2017.

THE STOCK SUPER CYCLE

For a longer-term perspective, I believe we can follow the Dow 1929 vs. NASDAQ 2000 predictor and say with confidence that the Dow will be relatively flat until about the year 2018, and then it will progressively move upward, similar to the 1990s rise of the stock market. Keep in mind that "relatively flat" is with respect to the semi-logarithmic chart previously presented (Figure 13). Flat in a semi-log scale of 10,000 is plus or minus several thousand points (in the 1964 to 1982 plateau of 1,000, it was several hundred points). This is the stock market Super Cycle of 18 years of plateau after 18 years of climbing. If there is a bear market, as I expect to see by late 2017 or early 2018, then I would stay out of the market until the bear has run its course – which could be up to two years or so, based on the average length of bear markets over the history of the Dow.

The stock market's last upswing of the Super Cycle was from 1982, the end of the last major inflationary cycle, until 2000 and the Y2K phenomenon. This was a time period when inflationary pressures were relatively low to almost nonexistent. Some analysts believe that the reason the stock market enjoyed such a long run of success was due primarily to low inflation rates. However, there is another theory that says low inflation rates did not cause the Dow to climb over 10,000. This theory has it that the stock market rise over the 1980s and 1990s was caused by stock repurchasing, stock options, and stock pension purchasing plans: "...after 1980, as has been stressed, the nonfinancial corporate sector as a whole was generally *buying and retiring* equities rather than issuing them."[96] The subsequent apparent "shortage" of stock availability then drives stock prices higher, due to supply and demand. In addition, the explosion of stock ownership pension programs (401k, 403b, and other tax deferred savings and investment plans) since 1981 has also contributed to the market's performance.[97]

THE NEXT BULL MARKET

The next Super Cycle upswing of the stock market will be an 18-year secular bull market from 2018 to 2036 that will see the market climb from 10,000 to 100,000. We don't yet know how low it will go as a result of the next recession, so I would definitely wait until there is some confirmation that the bear market is over before jumping back in. However, I do expect the 2020s to be a good time to be in the stock market. I also expect the first half of the 2030s to be healthy for the stock market, but I expect a peak of the market around 2036.

The 2020s will see a stock market boom the likes of which we have never seen before. It will be as momentous and significant as the 1990s or the 1920s stock market booms. Practically every day there will be new market highs. The stock market will become the topic of everyone's conversations. It will become the next media-mania topic. Every couple of years there will be a new 10,000-point barrier eclipsed. People will come to think that the market will always go up. Eventually, there will be a realization that the market is overpriced and, as with all bull markets, at some point the end will come. Whatever new innovation was driving the market in the 2020s will peak in popularity or saturate all possible opportunities, and the growth rate will slow or disappear. Whenever that point is reached and the majority of buyers realize they need to get out or get burned, the bubble will pop and the market will readjust. This readjustment will probably be painful, as in all speculative runs, and the people who have gotten in last will be the ones feeling the worst impact. Let's hope you are not one of them.

What will drive the market of the 2020s? The stock market boom of the 2020s will resemble in some ways both the 1990s and 1920s bull markets. It will be like the 1990s, in that I believe that innovation will drive the market, as the Internet did at the turn of the century. The challenges of energy and the environment will create opportunities for creative people all over the world, and this will provide a launching pad for new products that will make our lives less dependent on fossil fuels and our environment less subject to pollution and greenhouse gases.

I also believe that this next major market up cycle will be like the 1920s, in that it will occur in spite of and fully bearing the brunt of oppressive inflation. As I discussed in the prior section on inflation, the next up cycle of inflation will occur over the next 20 years. This will push the prices of everything up. The coming energy crisis, due to falling oil production, will drive prices of just about every consumer product on the planet. With this type of worldwide inflation, costs will rise, wages will rise, and stock market prices will rise. As inflation edges higher, you will want to be in inflation-hedged securities. In Stephen Leeb's book, *The Coming Economic Collapse: How You Can Thrive When Oil Costs $200 a Barrel*, he states that gold, oil, and real estate are where you will want to invest.[98] He calls them "Investment Jackpots" in his chapter, "Making Money in the Coming Collapse." I personally like real estate as an investment, but if you don't have the patience or ability to buy real estate, then Real Estate Investment Trusts (REITs) are also a good way to go. I believe real property (real estate) will benefit from a long inflationary period.

INFLATION AND THE STOCK MARKET

There was a long real estate investment boom in the early 1920s, as people throughout the country wanted to get a piece of the Sunshine State. The old joke about "I've got some swampland in Florida to sell you" comes from that era, as many hundreds, if not thousands, of people were purchasing Florida real estate, sight unseen. The "snow birds" were buying lots that were called "beachfront property" but were miles from the shoreline. As opposed to the California gold rush, Florida became the "Gold Coast," as so many fortunes were made on land speculation there. "Where the gold rush had drawn lone prospectors, Florida attracted whole families with grandparents and the family dog, all crammed into the Ford for the long journey south."[99]

Inflation was evident in many product prices in the 1920s, as it will be in the 2020s. Many art pieces were subject to higher prices, and so were other collectibles. In the 1920s, the upper class was very wealthy and took great care in displaying their wealth ostentatiously. Many ornate mansions were built in New York during this period, and the rich threw parties and balls to show off their immense wealth to each other. This was not limited to the houses or their persons; it included their pets.

Currently, there is an excess of capital in the market. This is called the "savings glut" in current business writings in newspaper articles and the financial news. This excess will drive the prices of assets, as people attempt to purchase "hard assets" for their cash before their money loses more (relative) value. Individuals will invest in gold, diamonds, and other precious metals and jewels, real estate, art, collectibles, and other tangible items. I expect the savings glut to also affect the stock market, in that people will continue to invest there, as opposed to leaving their cash in money market savings accounts that earn less than one-percent returns. I realize that, as inflation creeps higher, savings interest rates will also creep higher, but not at the same rate or level as the increase in prices for hard assets.

I believe the stock market will remain at its current level of around 10,000 (over 20,000 currently) through about 2018 (I expect the Dow to swoon from its current lofty heights down closer to 10,000 by the end of 2018). Then from 2018 to 2036, the Dow will climb steadily from 10,000 to 100,000. What will cause this order-of-magnitude increase? Inflation. I believe that inflation will cause the Dow to rise to new heights. This is counterintuitive: Everyone expects the stock market to do well in times of low inflation and not so well in times of high inflation.

There are multiple reasons why I think this. The first reason has to do with what was discussed earlier in the inflation section: We are coming to a time when worldwide production of oil will peak. This is called Hubbert's Peak, as already described. When the world experiences an inability to produce more oil to meet demand, shortages will ensue. Those shortages will drive up prices. Those prices will cause inflation, though inflation is usually considered bad for the stock market.

Low inflation, and its corollary – interest rates – have been seen as a factor in the 1990s stock market success. This was called the "Fed Model" in the 1990s, because Fed Chairman Greenspan had remarked that there was a negative correlation between stock market price-to-earnings ratios and the 10-year bond yield, meaning that, as the interest rate went down, the stock market went up. The theory went that, because bond yields were decreasing, more investors were turning to equities for higher returns. However, as Robert Shiller states in his book *Irrational Exuberance*, "...the evidence for the Fed Model is rather weak."[100] He goes on further to say that interest rates since 2000 have continued to remain low, but the stock market still suffered a significant decline. He also writes that, during the Great Depression, interest rates were low, but that did not improve or significantly impact the stock market.

In the future, severe gas and oil shortages will influence everything that is produced from a petroleum product or a petroleum by-product and will increase prices ten-fold. These increases in petroleum product-based prices will roll into the overall prices of everything in the economy. The Dow Jones Industrial Average of 100,000 will be more a reflection of inflation than any other effect. That level of inflation, and the interest rates it would take to rein in that runaway inflation, would probably put the Dow at a number roughly equivalent to what it is today.

However, if you don't aggressively manage your money to negate the effects of inflation, your savings and investments will not be enough to maintain your standard of living.

Also, it is not just cost-driven inflation that will challenge people's ability to maintain their standards of living but also the "wealth effect." As hundreds of millions of people in China and India become more affluent, the middle classes of both those countries grow. This will drive demand. As the demand side of products grows over time, prices will naturally increase (due to the law of supply and demand) over time.

LABOR SUPPLY AND THE STOCK MARKET

Not only will the demand side of the price/production curve drive prices but also the labor associated with that production will, too. With inflation due to rising gas and oil prices driving the cost of all basic goods, we also need to consider the wage aspect of costs. Workers will demand higher wages to pay for the increased cost of basic necessities. In addition, I am expecting a significant impact due to demographics. As an aging baby boomer, I expect to retire soon, and I am not alone. I was born in the late 1950s, which means I am part of the late boomers. The boom generation was from 1946 to 1964. Many of the earlier children in that population cohort, which resulted from the soldiers coming home from WWII, have already retired. Who is going to replace that workforce? I suspect the answer will be automation, but not everything can be automated.

I personally experienced this in the 1980s, when I started working in the aerospace industry. The aerospace industry has an 18-year cycle, which had bottomed out with the end of the space race in the early 1970s. Then there was a long interlude when most of the younger engineers were laid off (workforce reductions in aerospace were driven by a seniority system). For a while, very few engineers were hired. By the time I was hired by TRW in 1980, there was a significant age gap between the new hires and the next older employees. Then, the older engineers started to retire, which made the age gap increase and the demand for aerospace workers increase.

What I expect to occur in the near future is that, as the boomers retire, there will be a lack of skilled workers, which will drive a wage–price spiral, due to the supply/demand curve for a trained and highly skilled workforce. In addition, as inflation heats up and workers demand higher salaries to meet their needs, this will also add fuel to the fire of higher labor costs. Higher labor rates and higher salaries will drive higher prices for all products, but it will also provide additional capital for people to invest in the stock market. As people invest that same percentage of their pay in their 401k accounts, it will translate into more stock purchases and drive stock prices higher.

THE DOW 100,000

What will drive the Dow to over 100,000? I believe it will be inflation, in the sense that a dollar won't mean as much as it did in the past, so a stock price of $100 per share will be considered a low price point, as opposed to an "expensive" stock. Inflation will be propelled by the price of all consumables, as there will be shortages of water, food, and hard commodities in the future. This will be caused not only by an oil shortage, due to the implications of Hubbert's Peak and the eventual rationing or extremely high price of gasoline, but also by shortages of basic necessities driven by worldwide population growth.

The *Dow 40,000*, a book by David Elias, predicted that the Dow would reach 40,000 by the year 2016 – on June 2.[101] This book was written in 1998, during the Dow's climb from 1,000 to 10,000. He based this conclusion on an assumed 9% per year growth rate, which was a projection of the prior year's growth. The trouble is that this was a straight-line extrapolation of a short-term trend. I also believe the Dow will reach 40,000; however, I think Mr. Elias is off by a decade. My rationale for this belief is based on the 36-year stock market cycle I have described.

Since I have already stated my case for the Dow at 100,000, I expect people will be looking for more insight into what will happen when. The guidelines I will use for my own personal investing will be the following: 1) Expect the Dow to be within a few thousand points of the 10,000 mark by 2018 or so; 2) Expect a bear market of one to three years starting in late 2017 or early 2018; 3) The 2020s should be a great decade for stocks, like the 1990s or the 1920s; 4) Presume the Dow will gradually ramp up from the 10,000 range to the 100,000 range between 2018 and 2036; 5) Anticipate that the Dow will "flatten" out sometime around 2036. Look forward to the road being bumpy, with many ups and downs, but be prepared to take advantage of the opportunities as they present themselves. The year 2018 could be rough, as I expect it to be a recession year. In addition, 2017 could be very challenging for equities, as the stock market usually leads the overall economy by six months. I expect 2036 to be a momentous year – a "singularity" type of event, with the convergence of the peaks of three of the major cycles (inflation, the stock market, and business) – similar to the conditions prior to the 1929 Crash and the Great Depression.

This could be a repeat of the stock market climb to almost 400 in the early 1900s. At that time, the inflation cycle was also heading up, toward a peak that would occur around 1928. Then the Great Depression started after the stock market crash of 1929. We could see a similar depression after the stock market crash of 2036. Will this depression be as severe as the one in the 1930s? That would be difficult to predict, but the conditions will be similar, in terms of the cyclical patterns of inflation, real estate, the stock market, and the business cycle lining up in a similar fashion in phase to a time period of approximately 100 years ago.

After 2036, what will happen? Typically, what happens during the stock market secular bear cycle is that the market will level out and maintain the next 10th-order level (100 is 10^2, 1000 is 10^3, 10,000 is 10^4, and 100,000 is 10^5). It will resemble what we are seeing in the market now, with the Dow bouncing around the 10,000 (10^4) point. The Dow in that next secular bear market will bounce around the 100,000 (10^5) level. Then, when the brokers recommend a "buy and hold" approach to investing, you should tell them that you know better and invest your own funds. The winners during the secular bear cycles will be the people who jump in and out of the market, those who buy at the dips and sell at the peaks. After 2036, the losers will be the people who buy and hold.

Real Estate

We have all just witnessed the greatest bubble collapse in history. We are talking not millions or billions, but trillions of dollars worth of equity, wiped out. The real estate boom was worldwide, affecting property prices from Europe to the United States and the Far East. In 2012, prices were down 50% off their pre-2006 peak, and in some areas by as much as two-thirds. The rates of foreclosures have come down, but due to the severe reduction in property tax receipts in many cities across the nation caused by the nonpayment of property taxes and by people "walking away" from their homes, many cities have even gone bankrupt, the largest of which occurred to the city of Detroit, Michigan.

Only by understanding the duration and amplitude of the real estate cycle, which drives the financial health of many governmental institutions (particularly cities and counties, due to property taxes), will city planners, state controllers and other governmental budgetary authorities be properly prepared and armed to perform their fiduciary duties. I believe this is a critical circumstance that should be accounted for in the fiscal planning and budgeting of all municipalities.

In the following pages, I will describe some of the more recent peaks and valleys of the housing market, and what drove those changes. I will also show how these events fit a pattern, a periodic cycle, which can be used to determine what to expect in the coming years.

Chapter 9.
Tax Laws and Savings & Loans

Government deregulation occurred throughout the 1980s, as part of President Reagan's overall attempt to reduce the hand of government in business activities. He deregulated wage and price controls, the oil industry, the banking industry, and other government-controlled pricing mechanisms. President Reagan also reduced taxes, cut government domestic spending, and maintained strict control on monetary policy. This was called Reaganomics. "Reagan and his economic aides had brought about the largest spending-control bill, and the largest tax reduction, in American history."[102] I have already discussed the effects of monetary policy in the section on inflation. The point here is that all these effects are interrelated.

After the inflation monster was slain by Fed Chairman Paul Volcker in 1982, interest rates on loans came down. This allowed people to purchase higher-priced houses, because the lower rate meant a lower house payment for the same purchase price, or the same house payment for a higher-priced home (assuming, of course, you could afford the larger down payment, because 20% of a larger purchase price was still a larger down payment). Due to the reduction in regulations and to lax oversight, lending institutions were able to provide credit to questionable projects. This led to a boom in real estate prices and projects from 1982 through 1988. I will discuss the savings and loan deregulation effects later in this section.

The speculation in the housing market was also driven by the stock market. The stock market took a tumble in 1987, losing 500 points in a one-day debacle led by computerized trading. I remember being at work and feeling a palpable sense of fear from the people around me seeing their portfolios cut in half. The effect of all this was to cause people to pull money out of the market and put it into the "safe haven" of real estate. As it turns out, that was the exactly wrong thing to do. The stock market gained back those losses and went on to have the most incredible run of appreciation in history. In addition, the timing of that decision could not have been worse, because the real estate market peaked in January 1989. The other negative aspect of that unfortunate market timing is that real estate purchases are "sticky" – they are a lot less liquid and very time-consuming to get in and out of.

THE 1989 401K TAX LAW CHANGE

Tax law was also propelling the home-buying frenzy in 1988, at least in part. One of those tax law changes was the elimination of the 10% penalty for early withdrawals from 401k investment accounts, provided the withdrawal was for the purchase of a primary residence. This change helped fuel the boom in real estate; however, the sunset clause for that change was set to the end of 1988. This drove a purchasing rush, spiking real estate prices. I was one of the many who intended to use my 401k to fund the down payment for my first home. However, the market was such a whirlwind of activity, I had difficulty finding a property to buy. Every time we looked at a house, multiple offers were already in effect. It was very frustrating, and I was very unhappy with my realtor. Finally, a property in a less desirable neighborhood that had just fallen through escrow came up – and the realtor recommended we jump in.

So, I purchased a property in Lawndale, California, and it turned out to be a bad decision. Once the market turned sour – which it did, once the driving force for home purchasing was taken away (the law changed on January 1, 1989) – the bottom fell out. Housing prices were still driven by speculation, so the momentum continued through the first quarter of 1989, but by the summer of 1989, people could see that the bubble had burst. I purchased the house for $147,500. I refinanced in April 1989 to pay taxes on the withdrawal of my 401k funds, which had, in effect, a huge impact on my ordinary income, and the 1989 appraisal of my property was for $160,000. The property didn't exceed that valuation again for over 10 years. In fact, it fell to approximately $100,000 at the low point of the cycle, around 1995–1996. I know this explicitly, because my neighbors sold their house about that time, due to the death of their mother. The children sold the family home and split the proceeds, and the home sold at that price. Their house was almost identical to mine in square footage and lot size.

Looking back, I probably made one of the worst decisions in my investment career when I purchased a home with my 401k funds as the down payment. I paid a huge tax penalty that year ($15,000 in taxes and fees on the $26,000 used as the down payment). In addition, the subsequent decrease in the equity of that home, as I watched the price of neighboring houses go from $150,000 down to $100,000, basically meant that I had thrown that total of $41,000 away. On top of that, I probably could have purchased the same home a few years later for two-thirds the price. And the final blow? The stock market appreciation of that $26,000 during the same time period that I owned the home (from 1988 to 2004) would have completely blown away the eventual equity increase I obtained when I sold that property.

BECOMING A REAL ESTATE AGENT

The home-buying experience also had an effect on me personally. I was so disappointed and frustrated that I decided to become a real estate agent myself. I thought that I would be able to provide a better home purchasing experience to others than the one I had. I thought that, with my engineering background and my attention to detail, I would be able to provide a superior amount of information, along with better choices, than the average agent. And so I jumped in.

In December 1989, I completed my real estate training class and passed the state of California exam for my agent's license. With my newly minted license, I went to work as a part-time agent for a local real estate broker. I received additional training and was able to help a few friends from work find and purchase property in the area. I learned several lessons from this experience, one of which was to never do something half-way. As a part-time agent, I was never going to be able to dedicate enough time and energy to the effort it was going to take.

Another lesson I learned was, as in everything else, timing is everything. I happened to become a real estate agent just as the real estate market was diving headfirst into an ocean of problems. The savings & loan (S&L) scandals of the 1980s came to light in the late '80s and early '90s, and flooded the market with bad loans and debt. I struggled to sell anything (or even find clients) and wasted countless hours on the weekends at open houses where few, if any, people wandered in. As bad as it was, I felt worse for my broker, whose livelihood depended on those sales and client turnover. At least I had a full-time engineering gig to fall back on.

Then the recession of 1991 hit, and it got even worse. With manufacturing jobs moving to Mexico and other Latin American countries due to the North American Free Trade Agreement (NAFTA), workers were losing wage and benefit leverage. In addition, with the tearing down of the Berlin wall and the end of the Cold War in 1989, the aerospace sector was being significantly affected, particularly the disproportionate amount of aerospace and defense workers located in Southern California. These twin effects of both high-paying blue collar and white-collar jobs being lost at the same time in the same area made the real estate sector particularly weak in Southern California in the 1990s.

California was not the only region that saw real estate prices decline in the 1990s. Multiple local area markets lost significant value during that decade, and the real estate bubble popped for the East Coast (New York/New Jersey and Boston) and the South (Florida) in the United States, and for Japan. Japan was one of the worst hit economies due to the 1990s crash in real estate, and its subsequent decline lasted for years. The implementation of the Resolution Trust Corporation (RTC), a vestige of the 1930s housing decline, had a major impact on the liquidation of these "bad debts" in the United States. It provided a clearing of the S&L balance sheets and restored confidence in the market again.

Throughout the 1980s, Japan's manufacturing technology (and quality), business acumen (and methodology), and economic might were the envy of the world. It certainly seemed as if government and business leaders in the United States deferred to Japan for its ability to generate revenue and profit. Japan had used its manufacturing exports – in particular, automobiles, televisions, radios, and other consumer products – to become the second largest economy in the world. Japan also used its skyrocketing real estate values to go on a buying spree in the United States and other countries. Japan's property values at the peak of the bubble were about four times all of the land in the United States.[103] This was for a country that was smaller than the state of California. Using this leverage and the billions of dollars from their exports, the Japanese bought iconic US properties such as the Pebble Beach Golf Club in California, Rockefeller Center in New York City, and the National Broadcasting Corporation (NBC).

LINCOLN SAVINGS AND LOAN

By the early 1990s, the excesses of the 1980s real estate bubble in the United States were coming to light. Of particular infamy was the Charles Keating scandal. Keating owned the Lincoln Savings and Loan, and he used depositors' funds in a Ponzi-type scheme to defraud investors and retirees of their life savings. Keating took in millions of dollars from investors for high risk, uninsured bonds and used that money to invest in risky real estate ventures. As those risky ventures soured, Lincoln Savings came under investigation by federal banking regulators. Ed Gray, chairman of the Federal Home Loan Banking Board, was responsible for ensuring that thrift institutions stayed solvent and didn't end up costing taxpayers if they went bankrupt. Gray instituted new regulations imposing limits on the direct investments of savings and loans. He also doubled the number of audit regulators and increased their pay to reduce turnover. Keating tried to hire Gray away from the government to get him out of the way.[104]

The "Keating Five" as they were termed, consisted of five senators – John McCain (R-Arizona), Dennis DeConcini (D-Arizona), Alan Cranston (D-California), Don Riegle (D-Michigan), and John Glenn (D-Ohio) – who were convicted by the Senate Ethics Committee for providing political support to Keating in exchange for major contributions to their campaigns. These political favors gave Keating the appearance of government support and authorization. One of those favors involved running interference between Keating and Gray, and requesting the regulators "reach a compromise" with Lincoln Savings with regard to the property appraisals of their real estate assets. Their meeting in Washington with investigators examining the Lincoln case bordered on intimidation.[105]

Lincoln Savings and Loan wasn't the only thrift in trouble. Because of deregulation in the banking industry, many S&Ls throughout the country were either taken over by disreputable people or by honest people turned dishonest by the lure of easy money and the low probability of prosecution. One regulation change of particular note was the thrift ownership requirement: In April 1982, this requirement was changed from mandating a minimum of 400 shareholders, with no shareholder owning more than 25%, to allowing a single shareholder to own 100% of the S&L. As one could expect, this type of change brought out the worst in people and attracted the nastiest types to the S&L industry. As Pizzo, Fricker, and Muolo state in *Inside Job: The Looting of America's Savings and Loans*, "...many of the 'entrepreneurs' attracted by these changes were actually con men intent upon draining as much money from the system as they could and then moving on."[106]

SAVINGS AND LOAN DEREGULATION AND FRAUD

Deregulation went further for the state chartered thrifts, and the two worst states for potential fraudulent activity were California and Texas. In California, "...virtually anyone could own an S&L, attract as many deposits as he could pay for, and invest all those deposits in anything."[107] This was a result of the Nolan bill, which came about because all the California S&Ls were becoming federally chartered, and it was an attempt at regulation "parity" to compete for S&L business in the state. In Texas, the state thrifts were known for risk taking, deal making, and political schmoozing. In addition, Texas real estate was a hot market, because the oil industry was booming and oil prices had jumped 500% from the late '70s to the early '80s.[108]

One of the prime examples of excess and mismanagement of an S&L was Centennial Savings and Loan in Northern California. Centennial was run by Erwin Hansen, a former CEO of Far West Financial and a senior executive of Imperial Savings and Loan. In 1983, Hansen lent large sums of money to the executives of Centennial and booked those loans as profit, even though they were extremely inflated assets that would become underperforming and eventually end up in default. He also overpaid himself and the other Centennial executives, and provided them with additional perks like cars and parties paid for by Centennial.[109] In August 1985, Centennial was taken over by the government due to insolvency. It was one of the more expensive S&L failures, costing taxpayers $160 million.

Consolidated Savings Bank was another example of a badly managed S&L in California that ended up costing taxpayers over $100 million. However, these numbers pale in comparison to the Lincoln Savings and Loan. The damage done by Keating and his associates (mostly family and friends) was a federal bailout that cost taxpayers close to $3 billion.[110]

The California S&L industry was wide open and deregulated to the point of laissez-faire. But that was tame compared to the Wild West practices of the Texas S&Ls. Vernon Savings & Loan in tiny Vernon, Texas, had its own fleet of aircraft (a Falcon 50, a Lear Jet, multiple Cessna's, a King Air, and a helicopter). Its executives took extravagant vacations throughout Europe. Sunbelt Savings in Lubbock, Texas, held wild Halloween and Christmas parties in 1984 and 1985 that cost $1.3 million. By 1987, the Department of Justice had sent in a special task force to indict and convict the majority of these criminals. The government seized the records of 400 people from 30 thrifts in Dallas and the surrounding area. It was the largest white-collar crime probe in US history.[111]

Drug dealers, money launderers, mobsters, and racketeers all bought in to the S&L ownership bonanza and got away with unimaginable levels of theft, fraud, and embezzlement. The eventual burden on the US taxpayer was more than $300 billion. As Fricker, Pizzo, and Muolo state in *Inside Job*, "...deregulation had unleashed a holocaust of fraud upon the thrifts it had been designed to save."[112]

STOCK AND REAL ESTATE TRADEOFFS

The effect of the 1990s real estate meltdown probably aided the booming stock market in that same decade, due to those resources seeking higher returns. People take their assets in one market and apply them to another market. It is not unusual for this pattern to occur, as it has happened on multiple occasions in the past. The benefit of real estate is that you can use leverage quite easily – when you only put 20% down on a property and get a loan for 80% of it (the typical loan-to-value ratio), you are using leverage. Leverage is the use of other people's money to make money for you. In this case, the bank or savings and loan, which provided you the 80% loan, represents other people's money.

You can also buy stocks on margin, which is a leverage technique; however, that is not the typical way that people buy stocks, whereas carrying a mortgage is the typical way people buy real estate. Leverage also works in reverse, in that if you are leveraged in a real estate position and that real estate loses value, you could be "upside down" with your property, making it very difficult to liquidate the nonperforming asset. So, the two parameters you are trading off when you make a real estate investment versus a stock market investment are leverage versus liquidity. Real estate purchases have built-in leverage, because you only have to put down 20% of the purchase price and you can usually finance the rest. Stock market purchases have built-in liquidity, due to the sheer size of the stock market, both in terms of the number of stocks you can trade and the volume of trades occurring at any one time. The number of different stocks is in the thousands, and the volume of trading (the number of shares traded) is in the billions.

I chose the 1980s real estate bubble to show the "boom" times, and how government action (deregulation) and government inaction (lax oversight) can lead to trouble. It is an example of the rising wave portion of the real estate cycle, and was also my first experience in dealing with that cycle. The next chapter will provide an example of the downward phase of the real estate cycle. The real estate bubble of the 2000s was an excess caused by private sector greed, and it was also my second experience in dealing with the real estate cycle.

Chapter 10.
Derivatives and NINJNA Loans

After the 1980s real estate bubble, the next housing bubble started shortly after the stock market crash in 2000. People wanted a safe haven for their money, and it seemed like real estate would be it. They were correct for the next six years, but if they had understood the behavior and length of the real estate cycle, they would have known when the good times would end.

What enabled and drove the bubble was a financial creation called a derivative. A derivative is an instrument that is derived from the original asset or commodity. In this case, the real estate derivative was intended to be a hedge against the risk of real estate price declines. Ironically, the way these derivatives were packaged and sold to investors actually added risk to the system.[113] This invention has caused worldwide financial distress in communities, counties, states, and countries. It is at the fundamental core of the financial crises in several European countries, and it is the cause of several city bankruptcies throughout the United States, including one of the largest cities to ever declare bankruptcy – Detroit, Michigan.

The state of California had several cities declare bankruptcy in 2012: Stockton, Mammoth Lakes, and San Bernardino are some of them. Other cities are teetering on the edge of bankruptcy and have requested hikes to their sales taxes, in order to avoid bankruptcy: El Monte, Duarte, and Culver City are among those that were considering tax hikes in 2012.[114] The brand-new city of Jurupa Valley in Riverside County was also contemplating additional tax revenue.[115]

MY SECOND REAL ESTATE EXPERIENCE

As of the writing of this book, the country was still reeling from the excesses of the prior decade of cheap money and overinflated housing prices. I saw my own home rising in value at a rate of 25% per year, and like millions of other Americans, I was using it as an ATM machine to withdraw cash for improvements, cars, and vacations. I had read the entire *Rich Dad, Poor Dad* series of books and was looking for ways to get in on the action. I had missed out on the 1990s stock market boom, because the last real estate bubble had burned me in the late 1980s. I was afraid of buying in at the wrong time and had no idea when the stock market (which seemed like a bubble to me) would pop. A friend quoted an article from *Forbes* that said real estate had a 17-year cycle, and since the last peak was in 1989, that meant a peak in 2006. Unfortunately, I did not follow his advice.

I went ahead and bought rental property in Michigan in June 2004. It turned out to be THE worst investment of my life. I was under the misguided impression that I would be making about $1,000 per month, in total, for two properties. For my $100,000 investment, that would be about a 12% return, which seemed pretty good at the time. However, I miscalculated several things. First, I assumed the tax liability would be similar to that in California, which is 1% of the purchase price. It turned out to be more like 4% of the purchase price annually. Second, I gravely misjudged the maintenance costs to be approximately 10%, which turned out to be more like 25%, due to the age of the apartments. Third, I erroneously estimated the vacancy rate to be about 10%, and that turned out to be more on the order of 30%. All these factors combined to make my real estate venture the worst possible financial decision I could have made.

GREED AND SPECULATION

What drove the real estate bubble was a combination of cheap money and speculation. I remember reading articles in 2005 that described the new "real estate investment groups" – congregations of people who were meeting to discuss purchases of property, investment groups, locations that were hot, and the like. My boss at the time and his wife were involved in similar groups of friends investing in real estate. Every day he would tell me about how much money he was going to make on the condos he was purchasing in Phoenix, where people were buying the purchase contracts then selling the contract to other investors at huge profits. He was estimating that his contracts alone were worth hundreds of thousands of dollars.

In May 2005, *Fortune* magazine's cover page article was titled "Real Estate Gold Rush." This article covered four investors and their individual stories as they played out across the country from California to Florida, with stops in Las Vegas, Phoenix, and Austin, Texas. The interesting message the article conveyed was how speculative this real estate market was and how comparable it was to stock market speculation, especially day trading. The story described how many of these investors lost money in the stock market and were trying to recoup their losses in real estate.[116] They were all caught up in the excitement and lure of easy money, but the peak of this roller-coaster ride was only a year away. I don't know if *Fortune* ever went back to those people for a postmortem of how they fared after the fallout of the real estate bust, but that would have been an interesting read.

In June 2005, *Money* magazine dedicated one issue to real estate: the "Real Estate Guide 2005." Here the cover story was more about your home as an investment and how it was still a good time to buy. It wasn't as cautionary as the *Fortune* article. It stated that "...the Bottom is Unlikely to Fall Out." These articles discussed how hot the market was in San Diego ("Boomtown USA"), along with price forecasts, investment seminars, and creative financing.[117] Articles like these seemed to me to be pumping up the speculative real estate bubble. In *Irrational Exuberance*, Robert Shiller explains that the media added fuel to the fire of the stock market boom of the 1990s: "Given the heightened media coverage of investments, a stock market boom should come as no greater surprise than increased sales of the latest sport utility vehicle after a major ad campaign."[118] The same could be said of the real estate market of the early 2000s.

In December 2005, an article in *The New York Times* struck a more cautionary note; it was titled "Take It from Japan: Bubbles Hurt." It compared the real estate market in the United States with the real estate market from the 1980s in Japan. It told the story of a Tokyo city government employee who bought a small condo on the outskirts of town, because that was all he could afford. Then the Japanese real estate bubble burst, and he owed much more on the mortgage than the value of the unit. That put him in a situation where he couldn't move, because he could never sell for what he owed on the mortgage.[119] Does that situation sound familiar?

THE GREENSPAN PUT

I read another article, after the real estate bubble burst, which blamed the Fed chairman, Alan Greenspan, for the whole thing. It postulated that years of low-interest-rate loans produced the bubble, and that when he raised rates to slow the speculation, the bubble burst. This is akin to saying that companies that make sugar are to blame for people being fat. It just isn't true, and blaming one person's actions for the country's overall social and economic behavior is obscuring the facts. The true culprit of bubble-like behavior is the effect of capital flowing to areas of greatest return. And during the time phase of the housing cycle, when it is reaching the crest of the positive portion of the sine wave, more money gets invested, and as more money is invested, it appears to have higher returns, so then even more money gets invested. What is not accounted for is the amount of risk involved as the sine wave peaks and the potential for loss as the bubble bursts – this risk increases exponentially as you get closer to the peak of the boom.

The Greenspan "put" – which cites the extraordinary extent to which the Fed chairman went to ensure smoothly operating asset markets – was also blamed for the housing bubble. Since Alan Greenspan had overseen the Fed response to the stock market crash in 1987, a couple of months into his first term as Fed chairman, the market had looked to Greenspan to provide a cushion or "soft landing" if anything were to threaten economic prosperity or market stability and liquidity. In response to the stock market crash and the recession of 2000–2001, Alan Greenspan lowered the Federal Funds rate and kept the rate low through the middle of 2004. This move was seen as supporting evidence that the Fed chairman was intentionally inflating housing asset prices.[120]

As I have read more about the housing crisis and the creation of the investment vehicles that added fuel to the fire – credit default swaps and tranches that allowed subprime loans to collateralize, along with loans that are relatively secure, AAA-rated investments – I have learned that the housing boom was feeding on itself at the end. Alan Greenspan's raising of interest rates truly caused the end of the boom, but not in the manner in which he desired. He didn't want to pop the balloon, which is what eventually occurred; he wanted to cause a gradual decrease in the level of asset prices, which everyone knew were unsustainably high. This wasn't unique to America. Assets around the world were overpriced.[121]

GLOBAL EFFECTS

We went to Ireland to visit relatives in 2007, and they were talking about their real estate prices as if they would always go up. The relative who owned the bar in town was trying to buy out another relative who owned property across the street (which also happened to be oceanfront property). The amount of money these properties were going for was astounding, and then when you put the exchange rate on top of it, it was unreal. It seemed as if even the smallest properties in the area were priced at more than a million dollars, and this was a rural area that, while scenic, did not seem to me to be worth the million and multimillion dollar amounts that were being discussed. While we were there, we also watched television shows about real estate and home improvement that appeared to be on every channel. There seemed to be no end to the real estate frenzy and no way to satiate the demand for it.

Robert Shiller, in his book *The Subprime Solution*, shows how parallel the housing prices were on opposite sides of the Atlantic, with a graphic on London versus Boston homes. Furthermore, he goes on to state that the housing bubble of the early 2000s was a global phenomenon. In addition, both sides of the Atlantic had price decreases in the 1990s, reflecting a parallelism in the real estate crash of the late 1980s. In other graphs and descriptions, Shiller demonstrates that, in cities across the US, the same pattern exists – that is, the peak of real estate prices in one wave in the late 1980s, and the peak of real estate prices in a second wave in 2006. This data supports the information I described above in the two chapters on the 1988 peak (Chapter 9) and the 2006 peak (Chapter 10), which show that the overall real estate cycle's peak-to-peak value is about 18 years. See Figure 14 below, which shows peak prices in Boston in 1987 and 2005, and peak prices in London in 1988 and 2006.[122]

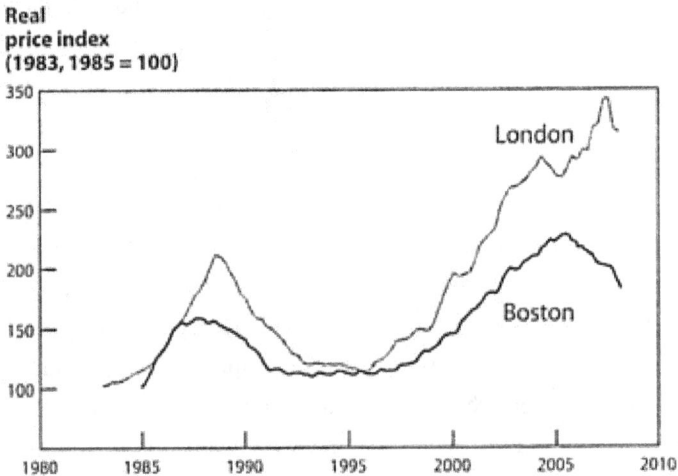

Figure 14. London and Boston Home Prices (1983-2008)

Shiller also wrote a classic book titled *Irrational Exuberance* in 2000, which correctly called attention to the stock market bubble of the late 1990s: "...the present stock market displays the classic features of a *speculative bubble*: a situation in which temporarily high prices are sustained largely by investors' enthusiasm rather than by consistent estimation of real value."[123] In its second edition, published in 2005, he included a new chapter (Chapter 2, The Real Estate Market in Historical Perspective) where he called attention to the potential bubble in the real estate market. This additional chapter was once again prescient, in that the real estate market peaked in 2006. Shiller has a knack for recognizing asset bubble situations, documenting the issue with appropriate graphics and data, and publishing the results. He is the author of the Case-Shiller Index of Housing Prices, which is now owned and published by Standard & Poor's.

CREDIT DEFAULT SWAPS

From the vantage point of the chief executive, President George W. Bush states (in his memoir *Decision Points*) that the cause of the real estate financial meltdown was the use of credit default swaps, the financial implementation of a derivative. Investment banks and financial firms sold volumes of types of these derivatives, known as collateralized debt obligations (CDOs). These mortgage-backed assets were also sold by quasi-government agencies Fannie Mae and Freddie Mac, which investors assumed had the full backing of the US government. However, that perception or implication was not real, until the decision was made to save these government-sponsored enterprises (GSEs) to the tune of about $100 billion each (eventually, that number was revised upward to $200 billion each).[124]

The reason these credit default swaps were so toxic was because banks and mortgage brokers were making loans to people who had no business owning homes. These were the NINJA (or NINJNA, for No Income, No Job, No Assets) loans, and they were all driven by greed. The mortgage brokers were getting commissions based on ever-increasing loan amounts. The finance people were making money by combining the toxic NINJNA loans with average and high-quality loans in tranches of mortgage-backed securities that would provide a high return on the bond with a reduced amount of risk. The risk was theoretically lowered, because the assumption was that not all subprime mortgagors would default at the same time.

The worst part of the equation was that none of the banks had any idea of who owned the toxic assets, because all these loans had become shredded and distributed in these derivatives as fractions or shares of loans, so nobody could assess or identify true owners or assign culpability if the loans went bad. This is why the resolution of the 1990s real estate crash was so much different from the most recent one. In the 1990s, your local savings & loan probably lent you the funds to purchase the real estate. However, this time there were so many different banks and so many different securitizations of the loans that no one had any idea who controlled the asset. Therefore, no one knew whose asset was now worthless, because both the owner and the debtor were literally unidentifiable.

At the peak of the financial crisis, the stock market fell to less than 7,000 in January 2009 – a drop of about 50% from its high of around 14,000 in October 2007. President Obama was inaugurated on January 20, 2009, and one of his first actions was to propose the $831 billion American Recovery and Reinvestment Act of 2009 (ARRA). This law, passed by Congress in February 2009, was the largest stimulus bill in US history. It was modeled after the New Deal that President Franklin D. Roosevelt enacted in the 1930s to fight the Great Depression. The ARRA addressed four main areas: energy, health care, education and the economy. It was a combination of tax cuts, subsidies, guarantees, and benefits.[125]

It has been over ten years since the peak of the last real estate cycle in 2006, and more than eight years since the end of the Great Recession in 2009. Janet Yellen replaced Ben Bernanke as the Federal Reserve Board Chair. Because the real estate bubble of the 2000s caused the Great Recession of 2007–2009, I have a new appreciation for former Fed Chairman Bernanke. It is ironic that his doctoral thesis was on the Great Depression, which seems to have uniquely prepared him to handle the crisis of the decade and quite possibly the worst financial crunch since the Great Depression. He was the right person in the right place at the right time to manage the situation, and he performed admirably. I think we all owe that man a debt of gratitude for his service to our nation.

These last two chapters have covered the last two boom and bust cycles in real estate, a period of about 40 years (from the 1980s to the current time). From my own personal experiences, I have come to realize the existence of the real estate cycle, and I am now painfully aware of the length of that cycle. The next chapter will delve into evidence of the time period and regularity of the real estate cycle.

Chapter 11.
The Real Estate Cycle

The real estate cycle is approximately 18 years long. I have personally experienced this, having purchased property near the peaks of both of the most recent booms. I bought my first home in 1988 during the prior real estate boom (which peaked in November or December 1988, but momentum carried it into 1989), and I purchased rental property in 2004, near the last real estate peak in 2006.

There can be no argument about whether or not there is a real estate cycle, as evidence of it abounds, and in one way or another, it has affected almost everyone. The only argument about the real estate cycle can be in its length or duration. The purpose of this section is to present the case I propose as to its length of 18 years. Just because the most recent evidence regarding the real estate cycle has been 18 years long, should we expect the next peak to be 18 years after the 2006 peak? The answer is yes, because the real estate cycle has been that long, on average, for the last 100-plus years.

In an article titled "The Great 18-Year Real Estate Cycle," Steve Hanke posits that peaks in land values, housing construction, and the business cycle are highly correlated. He references a table from Dr. Fred Foldvary's *The Depression of 2008*, which I show below as Figure 15. Hanke states: "These data talk, and the most interesting thing they say is that every 18 years we can expect the culmination of a credit-fueled real estate and ensuing business cycle. This, of course, doesn't imply that all recessions are preceded by a real estate cycle. It only says that all real estate cycles have spawned economic downturns."[126] The most interesting thing from my perspective is how regular and consistent this cycle is (see the second column interval values).

The Great 18-Year Real Estate Cycle

Peaks in Land Value Cycle	Interval (years)	Peaks in Construction Cycle	Interval (years)	Peaks in Business Cycle	Interval (years)
1818	-	-	-	1819	-
1836	18	1836	-	1837	18
1854	18	1856	20	1857	20
1872	18	1871	15	1873	16
1890	18	1892	21	1893	20
1907	17	1909	17	1918	25
1925	18	1925	16	1929	11
1973	48	1972	47	1973	44
1979	6	1978	6	1980	7
1989	10	1986	8	1990	10
2006	17	2006	20	December 2007	18

Figure 15. The Great 18-Year Real Estate Cycle[127]

REAL ESTATE PERIODIC CONSISTENCY

What is missing from this table is the time period between the peak of real estate prices in the 1920s and the peak in the 1970s. This 50-year gap includes the Great Depression in the 1930s, World War II in the 1940s, the housing boom after the veterans came back from war the 1950s, and the civil rights/Vietnam War/space race era in the 1960s. I don't agree with Dr. Foldvary that there was no peak of real estate prices during this time period. I believe there was variability in property prices, including peaks during the Depression, and that there was a significant real estate boom during the 1950s, as people competed for housing in the postwar era. Data from Robert Shiller's *Irrational Exuberance* spreadsheet for home prices perfectly fit a bottomed-out real estate cycle in 1933 and spiking real estate prices in 1940. Then, in the early 1950s, prices jump due to GIs coming back, starting families and buying homes (showing a supply/demand jump in aggregate prices). I also disagree with Dr. Foldvary about the length and peaks of the business cycle, but that topic will be discussed in Section IV.

Dewey and Dakin, whose book *Cycles: The Science Of Prediction* was published in 1947, had definitive statements on the 18-year real estate cycle with respect to the Great Depression years through World War II and the return of the veterans. They stated that real estate boomed from the end of World War I in 1919, peaked in 1925, and then dropped to a low point in 1933. Falling real estate prices had been accelerated by the onset of the Depression in the early 1930s, but by 1933, prices had stabilized. The next upswing of the real estate cycle was launched with the implementation of the New Deal and all the government programs it instituted.[128]

Dewey and Dakin further stated that government activity in the building of public works for dams, power plants, and other major infrastructure improvements added to the volume and breadth of the real estate upswing. Building activity peaked in 1940, after which the United States became involved in World War II in 1941. With the outbreak of war, "...building of homes and farm structures had to cease almost entirely, under government decree – the famous L-41 regulation of the War Production Board."[129] However, after the end of the war, there was so much pent-up demand and a "swollen mass incomes" that the next upswing of the real estate cycle was inevitable.[130]

THE MASTER PLANNED COMMUNITY

Since Dewey and Dakin's book was published in 1947, they had no way of knowing that the end of the war would usher in a whole new era in building and real estate to respond to the postwar building crisis – the lack of homes for all the new families created by servicemen and women returning home to start their postwar lives. The response to that demand was the invention of the "master planned community" in Levittown, New York.

Levittown was named after its builder, Levitt & Sons; Abraham Levitt was the founder of the company, and his two sons, William and Alfred, were its salesman and architects, respectively. It was the first suburb built with mass production-type construction and methodology in response to the dire need for housing for veterans that resulted from the restrictions on residential housing construction during the war years. William Levitt, who served in the Navy during the war, gained valuable experience in the prefabrication and mass-production of military housing, which used uniform and interchangeable parts, like the building of a car or an airplane on an assembly line. [131]

When the brothers returned to the family business after the war, they used their experience building military housing to mass produce residential housing. They used precut lumber and interchangeable parts, and built the houses on slab foundations – a rare approach at the time. In fact, they needed a change to the building code in Nassau County in order to build on a slab foundation. They also used nonunion workers but provided incentives and high wages to keep their employees satisfied. The original 2,000-unit community was wildly successful, and they quickly expanded operations to other areas around the country. The Levitt's are credited with creating the first master planned community, complete with amenities such as a community center, a swimming pool, and common areas. These houses were modern, had hot water radiant heating systems, and started at only $7,990.[132]

From the peak of the postwar housing boom in 1955 (which is shown by Shiller's Home Price Index), home prices generally declined until about the mid- to late-1960s. Then home prices climbed at a rapid rate and peaked around 1972. The severe recession of 1973–1974 negatively impacted housing prices, but by the late 1970s, home prices were surging again, mostly due to the effect of severe inflation. The next peak in the real estate market occurred in 1988–1989, as I have discussed in prior sections.[133]

THE KUZNETS BUILDING CYCLE

Many economists and academics have recognized the existence of the real estate cycle. The work of Simon Kuznets is particularly notable, as he is credited with identifying the 15–25 year "building cycle" that is now generally referred to as the Kuznets wave. This wave is associated with the construction cycle and is related to the real estate home building wave. However, the evidence from various sources fixes the real estate cycle at 18 years. Since the building cycle is so long, it is not easily discernable by most business people, and most people don't see it in their careers more than once because most business careers are less than 40 years. I would think that most people would see one wave and not think about it nor recognize the second one, because it is so long since the last one.

Recent analysis has suggested a more definitive relationship between the Kuznets (infrastructure) and Kondratieff (Long Wave) cycles. In a paper titled "Spectral Analysis of World GDP Dynamics: Kondratieff Waves, Kuznets Swings, Juglar and Kitchin Cycles in Global Economic Development, and the 2008–2009 Economic Crisis" by Andrey Koroyatev and Sergey Tsirel, the authors show the relationships between Kuznets cycles and Kondratieff waves.[134] They also fix the Kuznets cycle at 17–18 years, versus the 15–25 years referenced in other works. "Incidentally, the respective period (17–18 years) is quite congruent with the one initially discovered by Kuznets."[135] Thus we can see that, akin to the relationship between the Kitchin and Juglar cycles for the overall business cycle (three Kitchins for every Juglar cycle, see Section IV), there is a similar relationship between Kuznets and Kondratieff cycles (three Kuznets for every Kondratieff cycle). In addition, the Kuznets swings are tied to demographics and the influence that those changes have on building and construction. As people migrate among countries or in and out of generational cycles, there is a natural, biological rhythm to it.

GENERATIONAL EFFECTS

The fact that the real estate cycle is a generation long is no accident. It takes time for people's memories to fade and for people to get over the last bubble. In addition, a generation (about 18 years) is the amount of time for each successive parent-child relationship to advance to the point where new dwellings are required. I realize this is an oversimplification, but the point is clear. The generational aspect of the real estate cycle is real. Children are born, and family size grows and then shrinks as kids go to college. Then they get married and start the cycle over again, so there is a natural rhythm to the whole process. And even though people are getting married and having children later in life, there is still the aspect of children moving out of their parents' homes to make lives of their own.

Dewey and Dakin, in *Cycles: The Science Of Prediction*, state that there is an 18-year cycle in real estate, construction, and building: "...this 18-year rhythm seems one of the cleanest, most regular patterns revealed in our economic life."[136] Dewey and Dakin also state that the evidence shows this 18-year cycle goes back to the 18th century, from the results of research on the number of bricks produced in England, according to tax records. They also show graphs of real estate development in Chicago and New York City. The figures show that most of the skyscraper building occurs at the peaks of the real estate booms, probably driven by the availability of cheap financing during times of prosperity. What is interesting is that these figures also show that John D. Rockefeller in New York and William M. Wrigley in Chicago seemed to understand the 18-year cycle; they started construction on their buildings during the low points of the cycle, so that the buildings were fully rented by the time construction was completed.[137]

HOUSING METRICS

Housing starts is just one metric observed on a regular basis in the financial news, and it provides a barometer on the health of the economy. In 2006, real estate was a significant part of the economy, due to the emphasis on new house construction, home improvement, refinancing, and all the other aspects of the real estate boom. A large portion of the employment figures was tied to real estate, for construction workers, real estate brokers, mortgage brokers, home improvement employees (at retailers like Home Depot and Lowes, for example), and other related industries. Merrill Lynch estimated that by 2005, real estate was driving US GDP growth: "More than half of all new private-sector jobs since 2001...were in housing-related activities." [138] When the real estate sector nosedived, employment figures in the state of California and across the country nosedived, too.

Both new home sales and new home construction show a dramatic increase in the years following the natural decline from the prior peak in the late 1980s. These data do not include the volumes for sales of existing homes. The data are from the US Census Bureau and are seasonally adjusted. The data cover a span of about 50 years (all that is available from their website). What is significant is the unprecedented number of new homes (single family residences – SFRs) sold in this most recent real estate bubble. From these data, I have created Figure 16, which shows that the sales of new SFRs peak at about 1,400,000 in June 2006, about 500,000 more than any prior peak in history. This is part of what made the housing crisis so unprecedented; the volume of sales was 50% more than at any other time in US history.

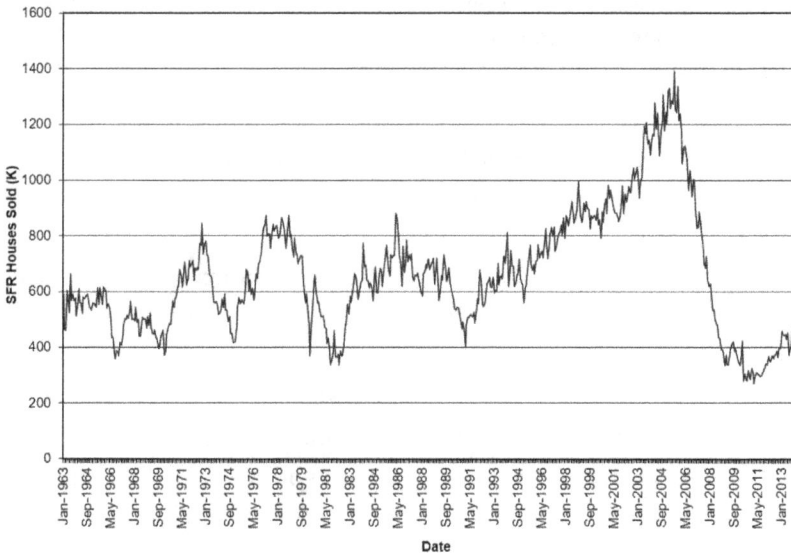

Figure 16: New Home (SFR) Sales (1963-2013)[139]

AN EMOTIONAL INVESTMENT

When real estate is booming, the people who own property are very happy. They talk about how much money their house is making while they sit at home. They feel richer and more confident in the future, because of their paper wealth. Sometimes, they brag to their friends about how their $500,000 home is now worth $1.5 million, even though they would never sell the property to realize that gain. All the while, the people who don't own property feel awful. They say they should have bought in a few years ago, when prices were more reasonable and they could actually afford it. Now they feel as if they've missed the opportunity and are standing next to that escalator, watching people rise above them, while they remain on the ground. They may even become somewhat desperate, feeling as if they have to jump in now or risk never being able to qualify to own a home.

I have personally experienced both of those emotions, as having been through both of the most recent real estate cycle peaks. It is a terrible feeling to jump into a situation out of desperation – thinking that it's your last opportunity to buy, only to find out you could have purchased that same property for 30% less if you had only waited a few years. It is also a terrible feeling watching your millionaire status disappear as the housing bubble bursts, taking your dreams with it. If only you had made the right decisions at the right time, you could have saved yourself a lot of fear, grief, anxiety, and self-loathing.

What you need to understand is that you can make the right decisions, if you are armed with the right information, so you can be prepared when those opportunities in life present themselves to you. The real estate cycle will come around, and it will offer those choices that can make you rich, if you choose. As I have stated before, the real estate cycle, like the other cycles I have described in other sections of this book, will provide opportunities to "get in" when the conditions are optimal for your future benefit. But you need to have the correct information in front of you, so you can make that informed decision. You need to have the information I will present in the next chapter, which will provide a summary of the expected events in the near and long term that will determine when the next opportunity will arise to buy into the American Dream.

Chapter 12.
What's Next for Real Estate

As already noted, money moves to the site of highest returns. In 1987, when the stock market took a dive and people were looking for a place to put their money to work, real estate was almost peaking and providing a high return on investment. It happened again, in 2000 and 2001, when the stock market crashed and people started to take their money out of the stock market and invest in real estate. The next opportunity for this to occur will be the next drop in the stock market. As noted in the stock market section, this drop will probably happen by the end of 2017.

If the peaks of the last two real estate cycles were in 1988 and 2006, and the cycle is 18 years long, then the next peak will be in the year 2024. I believe that this peak will be driven by inflation. In addition, the following 9-year business cycle (discussed in depth in the next section) will peak about 2023, and that will affect the real estate cycle (the recession phase of the business cycle usually negatively impacts the real estate cycle). The real question is, since the next inflation peak will not occur until 2036, what else will drive real estate prices back down? As you have already seen in the stock market section, I believe that the stock market will be booming at that time, and money – always seeking the highest returns – will move from real estate to stocks.

The next driving factor for real estate prices will be inflation. As inflation goes higher, the value of hard assets – gold, commodities, and real estate – will rise. I have already defined the cycle for inflation as being the 54-year Kondratieff cycle, and the upward portion of that cycle has started or will be starting soon. The inflationary cycle, like a rerun of the 1970s, will put pressure on real estate prices throughout the country and probably in the rest of the world. This is good news for the millions of property owners who are currently underwater on the value of their properties – their mortgage obligations are larger than the current value of the properties. Hopefully, most of those people have refinanced to a fixed-rate mortgage, because interest rates, like inflation, have only one way to go – up!

INFLATION AND REAL ESTATE

I believe we will see a replay of the 1970s, with a gas crisis, inflation, higher interest rates, and a stagnant economy. Hopefully, with knowledge of the past applied to this new reality, we will be able to endure those hardships and minimize the impact these issues will have on the economy and our society as a whole. Inflation, as good an effect it has in terms of the appreciation of home values, tends to have overall negative impacts on people's attitudes and prospects for the future.

There will be two trends that play against each other, as the next decade unfolds, with respect to real estate. The first trend will be inflation. Inflation will drive the price of real property – real estate, commodities, and the like – higher and higher over the next several years. The counterpoint to this trend will be interest rates. As inflation goes higher, so will interest rates. As interest rates climb, mortgage payments will increase, so the affordability factor becomes a major issue in people's ability to pay for more expensive homes and housing in general. This could become a challenge to the overall factors driving prices higher (the demand side).

The Fed's credit easing and economic stimulus led to the lowest interest rates in over 50 years. As this stimulus unwinds over the next few years, interest rates will rise. Rising rates will challenge the real estate market and drive prices lower, or at least flatten the current trend. From 2012 to 2013, home prices rose 10%–20% in some areas, causing some pundits to declare the end of the real estate bust of 2008. However, this rise was driven by the economic stimulus of the Fed, which drove mortgage interest rates below 4%.

There has already been a surge in real estate prices, driven by the Fed's moves to provide long-range stability and lower interest rates in the 30-year loan arena through the Treasury purchase program (at $40 billion per month). This strategy has significantly reduced the amount homeowners have to pay for their mortgages. With cheaper mortgages, homebuyers can afford higher priced homes, so the effect of the Fed's action is to raise prices for all homes.

THE STOCK MARKET AND REAL ESTATE

When the stock market makes its next correction and returns to the mean, investors in search of higher gains will once again discover the real estate market. This will drive a renewed zeal for the property market. However, there is a bigger reason why investors will start investing in real estate again: inflation! Inflation will drive real estate values through the roof (no pun intended), as real property holds its value much better than paper assets, like stocks and bonds, during an inflationary period.

I believe that real estate prices will continue to go up, driven initially by low interest rates and then subsequently by inflation. I believe that inflation will dominate our lives in the future, because of the impending effect of Hubbert's Peak. Property prices will rise because ALL prices will rise. The lubricant of our current economy is oil. Whoever has oil will dominate the marketplace and the international stage. Those countries that are oil importers may need to import their oil from places closer to them. Those countries that are oil exporters may find that they have more leverage, both from a contracting and a negotiating point of view.

How much will prices go up? Will they go up as much as in the last real estate bubble in 2006? I think the answer to that question is yes. During the last four years of the most recent growth of the real estate market (2002–2006), prices climbed at an average rate of 25% per year in many real estate markets. I expect a 100% increase in the price of housing by the end of the next cycle, the end of 2024. The question you have to ask yourself is: Is the house I am now living in the right place, or will there be a change in the near future that will make me reconsider the location I currently reside in? If the answer to that question is yes, then you should consider timing your purchase, such that it does not occur during the peak years of the next housing boom (2020–2024).

Of course, no decision should be made out of context or in direct conflict with current events. You need to be aware of your surroundings and the economic state of affairs of the country, your region, and your own personal status. I believe that now is the right time to purchase real estate, as the intersection of interest rates and market prices may not continue to favor owning versus renting, as it currently does. With the expected housing price increases due to inflation and the expected interest rate increases the Fed will have to impose in order to curb that inflation, future housing costs will be much greater. The Federal Funds rate, currently hovering around 0%, is as low as it could ever be and is the lowest it has ever been. Interest rates can only go up. As shown on the chart in Figure 17, there is a cycle to the Fed Funds rate that approximates the Kondratieff cycle. The low of 0.68% occurred in 1958, rising to a peak of 19% in 1981 and then returning to a low of 0.07% in 2012 (low to low, versus peak to peak). Thus, we are currently enjoying a "sweet spot" of low interest rates and relatively low prices for real estate.

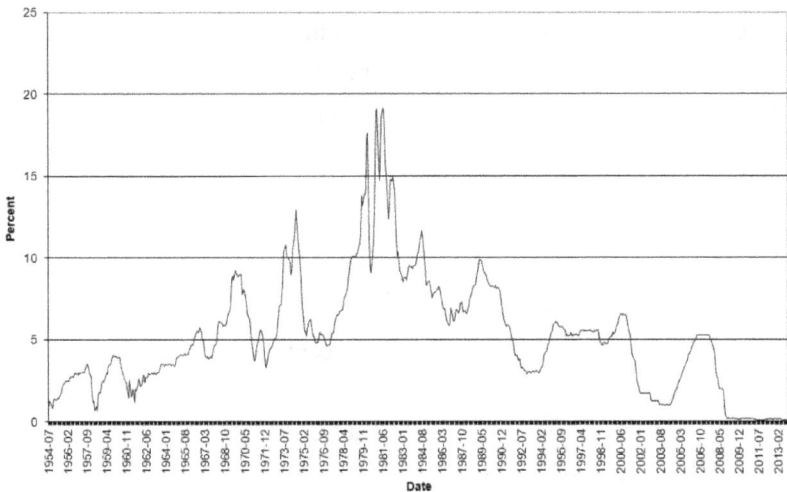

Figure 17. Fed Funds Rate (1954–2013)[140]

REAL ESTATE PRICES

Prices are still down from their 2006 highs, so I believe there is "cap room" for additional increases in real estate prices even before inflation takes hold. A November 15, 2013, article on MarketWatch.com showed the five states with the largest decreases in home values (in absolute terms, not percentages) – as you might expect, they were California, Nevada, Arizona, Florida, and Maryland. Nevada's and Maryland's home prices were driven by Las Vegas and Washington, DC, respectively. The article went on to state that "home values would need to rise another 26% in Los Angeles County and another 53% in Riverside-San Bernardino in order to reach their 2006 peak, says Dutra. 'We don't foresee that happening in the next five years,' he says."[141]

I don't believe we will see these types of home purchasing conditions – low interest rates and relatively cheap prices – for another 60 years. We are at the cyclical inflation and interest rate low for the century; we are also experiencing a low in cyclical home prices for the current real estate cycle. My recommendation would be to invest in real estate with fixed-rate loans, and expect that home prices and rents will eventually rise. Remember always that the three most important words in real estate are location, location, and location. Also consider the likely scenarios that ocean levels will rise in the next 15 to 30 years and that low-lying areas may be underwater in the next decade or so. In addition, the US population is expected to increase by almost 100 million, to over 400 million people, by the year 2050, and the majority of that increase is expected to be in cities and suburban areas.

What this amounts to is a recommendation that larger cities and metropolitan areas that are not threatened by rising sea levels should be the best places to invest. In particular, places in the Sun Belt, which tend to become retirement sites for graying America, should provide the most favorable opportunities. Las Vegas, Phoenix, Dallas, and Atlanta are areas that saw a significant decline in home prices in the recent real estate bust, and they should see a recovery in those prices. I also think that the Sun Belt and Southwest are ideal places to invest in, due to climate change. As extreme weather gets worse over time, there will be a continued migration of people leaving the North and East to live in the South and West.

Multiple factors drive real estate prices: interest rates, unemployment rates, population expansion, new housing starts, foreign investment, and so on, and these factors are interconnected and related to each other. We have already discussed the connection between interest rates and unemployment in the section on inflation (Section I), and those two factors were shown to be inversely correlated; that is to say, high interest rates are typically associated with a period of low unemployment, and low interest rates are typically associated with a period of high unemployment. Subsequent paragraphs will discuss the effects of population, new housing, and foreign investment on real estate prices and activity.

REAL ESTATE DEMOGRAPHICS

I don't necessarily subscribe to the notion that the demographics of the baby boom generation will drive future home prices, as I believe that trend is being driven by other factors. However, other demographic changes may affect housing prices. As the US increases its total population from over 300 million to over 400 million in the next few decades, there will be a shift in the general makeup and diversity of the American people. At that time, America will actually be younger and more ethnically diverse. There are other demographic changes that may surprise people, and these are detailed in *The Next Hundred Million: America in 2050*, a book by Joel Kotkin. He writes that more people will move to the suburbs and out of the city due to the Internet, which allows people to work anywhere.[142] This conflicts with my own personal view that cities will become denser as people move closer to their jobs to avoid transportation costs, due to the coming oil crisis.

The population of the United States is still growing, in stark contrast to those of Japan and some countries in Western Europe, which have low birth rates and negative population growth – a higher death rate than birth rate. In addition, this condition could accelerate as the population's average age increases over time. The point of these comments is that we should expect the prices of real estate to rise over time, continuing on the path of a sine wave with a negative slope, which looks like a wavy staircase going up at a low rate, perhaps 5% per year.

New housing starts will continue to increase; however, the rate of this increase will be proportional to the amount of funding available for investment and to a business environment that is favorable to financing. Currently, the capital markets are overflowing, and money is available and cheap. Financing terms are generally advantageous, but keep in mind that there are stricter guidelines and more red tape to go through to get approved. Risk-averse banks and financial institutions are less likely to authorize new development projects without the pedigree of established firms. What this means for new housing construction is that projects will be more heavily scrutinized in the future, before funding is approved. This will result in inventory lower than the industry's capacity – employment in this very hard-hit sector will continue to be sporadic and hard to get. But it will improve over the next decade (see Figure 18).

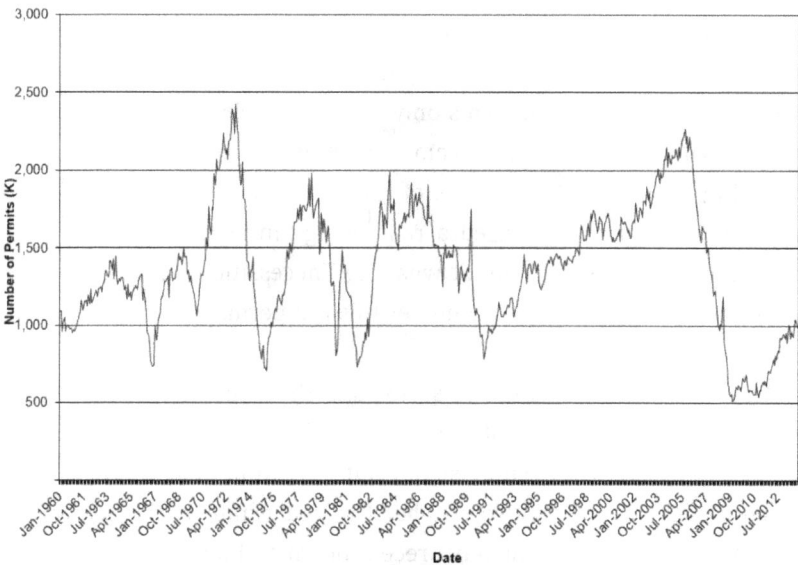

Figure 18. New Housing Starts (1960–2013)[143]

Foreign investment is directly affecting the current housing market. In many cases, overseas investors, mostly Chinese, looking for the safety and security of US real estate, are making all-cash deals. Since the US real estate market has already recovered somewhat from the gloom and doom of the 2008 financial meltdown, it has become attractive to external entities. The Chinese are drawn to high-end properties in established neighborhoods, with good local education and ethnic (typically Asian) communities. The affluent Chinese seem particularly interested in $1.0 million– $1.5 million properties in newer neighborhoods. Since the ownership of property is celebrated here as in no other country, the United States will continue to be a focal point and magnet for foreign direct investment (FDI).

REAL ESTATE BOOM POSTMORTUM

We have all witnessed the carnage of the real estate bubble, which burst in 2006 and then plagued the financial markets for the next several years. The number of people with upside down mortgages was staggering. Many people had purchased at or near the peak of the bubble, expecting the good times to last forever. Lots of people (including myself) used the equity in their home to pay for cars, boats, expensive vacations, and to pay off credit cards. This only added to their debt load and their misery when housing prices came crashing down and loan-to-value turned upside down. The depths of this "debt hangover" have affected millions of people and caused a real change in attitudes toward consumption and in feelings about what are "necessities" versus what are "luxuries." Only time will tell whether this is a permanent change in attitude.

In summary, the real estate sector and the housing market will rebound from this most recent bubble implosion, and prices will recover. Given time, there will even be significant growth in this sector, as inflation drives prices of real assets higher. The real estate market has an 18-year cycle that repeats. The most recent boom and bust cycle of the real estate market was dramatic to all and traumatic to many. It is this trauma that provides opportunity, in that many people have been burned by the experience and will be reluctant to dive back in. A lot of Americans have been experiencing a debt hangover and are weary of their prior real estate experiences. However, current price and interest rate levels are such that there may never be a better time to buy. Those who are positioned to take advantage of the opportunities that present themselves in the next boom cycle of the real estate market will be poised to earn great wealth – or at least not lose what they have to the ravages of inflation.

Business

The business cycle is a critical and fundamental element of macroeconomics. It is the basis of many economic decisions and the primary focus of articles or pieces in print media, radio, television, and the Internet. The term "business cycle" is ubiquitous and gets millions of hits when searched on Google. Even with all this interest and debate, the business cycle is still misunderstood. However, if you want to be successful in the personal and professional aspects of your financial life, you need to understand the business cycle.

The business cycle has different "seasons" – like the four seasons of the calendar year. First, there is recession – like the winter, it occurs at the "bottom" or end of the previous cycle. Second, there is recovery – like the spring, it occurs right after winter "with regularity," as Jim Rohn used to say. Third is the expansion – like the summer, it occurs in the middle of the cycle. The fourth and final season is the crisis – like the fall, it happens just before winter.

The business cycle is the shortest of the cycles I am describing in this book, at nine years. The next longest cycle, real estate, lasts about 18 years. The stock market has a 36-year cycle (though not a sinusoidal wave). And inflation has the longest cycle, called the Long Wave, which is typically 54 years. Note that all these cycle periods are multiples of the business cycle – 9, 18, 36, and 54 are all multiples of 9. This is an oversimplification, but it is a useful parameter that is easy to remember.

Chapter 13.
The Great Expansion

Expansions represent the upward phase of the business cycle. As such, they occur with the same regularity and the same periodicity as recessions, about every nine years. They correlate to several factors existing in the economy: available credit, plentiful labor, and benign inflation (although low inflation is not a requirement). Expansions are typically longer than contractions (recessions), per the National Bureau of Economic Research (NBER) data. An expansion is harder to detect, as people don't usually see its immediate effects, as they would with layoffs in a recession. Both recessions and expansions have definitions based on the direction of GDP (a percentage increase smaller or greater than in the last quarter).

In this book, I have written about The Great Inflation, The Great Depression, and The Great Recession. Others have coined all these terms, and all these events have a place in the collective conscious memory of the nation. Why aren't the opposite effects written about or memorialized? Why not call the 1990s "The Great Expansion" – as it should be remembered?

The 1990s saw the longest peacetime economic expansion in US history. Several economic factors combined to make this one of America's greatest decades. It was marked by low inflation and low unemployment. It was a time of increasing worker productivity and the application of technology to the country's problems. The Internet had a lot to do with this, especially during the latter half of the decade. It also had a lot to do with how computers became an integral part of everyday life. Computers were also behind what would become the biggest non-event of the 21st century – Y2K. I discussed Y2K relative to the stock market in an earlier section, but it is also relevant to the business cycle because of the economic expansion caused by millions of computer users upgrading their hardware and software for Y2K compliance.

ECONOMIC WINTER BECOMES SPRING

The end of the 1980s saw the end of the Cold War, and with it several thousand jobs in the aerospace and defense sector. In addition, there was a hangover from a long real estate binge, which caused many savings and loan institutions to fail, and that added job losses. By the early 1990s, these job losses and the effects of President Bush's tax increase took hold. By 1991, the economy was mired in a short recession, but that should have been expected, given the length of the prior business cycle and the effects of the real estate crash. In addition, race riots broke out in several large cities, due to the verdict in the Rodney King trial – white policemen in Los Angeles were found not guilty of any crime in the beating. The economy is what drove President Bush out of the White House.

The savings and loan (S&L) crisis and the end of the 1980 real estate boom strained the 1990s financial and real estate markets. As I wrote earlier in the real estate section, by the end of 1989, many properties were upside down (the outstanding mortgage debt was greater than the value of the property). The Resolution Trust Corporation (RTC) was a government organization responsible for dealing with the real estate crash of the late 1980s and liquidating billions of dollars of real estate. The RTC was effective in resolving the issues associated with the savings & loan scandal of the 1980s, in terms of S&Ls that had purchased their own portfolios of questionable real estate holdings and were forced to liquidate for pennies on the dollar (some for 50% or less than original values). The RTC was efficient in dealing with illiquid real estate, and it provided a great service.

At the turn of the 1990s, a new invention, the World Wide Web, was unveiled when Tim Berners-Lee created the first web page in 1990. By 1992, the term "surfing the Internet" was coined by Jean A. Polly.[144] In 1992, Arkansas governor Bill Clinton defeated President George H.W.

Bush in the November presidential election. Third-party candidate Ross Perot, a Texas billionaire, influenced the election by taking conservative votes from the Republican candidate Bush. President Clinton was a Rhodes scholar at Oxford and went to Yale Law School. He understood economics and used his law education effectively as president.

President Clinton also staffed his team with competent talent – Treasury Secretary Lloyd Bentsen served in Congress as the chairman of the Senate Finance Committee. The deputy treasury secretary was Roger Altman, an investment banker (Blackstone Group) and President Carter's assistant secretary of the Treasury. Clinton's budget director was Leon Panetta, who chaired the House Budget Committee in the California Congress, and his deputy was Alice Rivlin, an economist and deficit "hawk." He asked Robert Rubin, former Goldman Sachs co-chairman, to become chair of the National Economic Council (NEC). Clinton selected Laura Tyson, an economics professor from UC Berkley, as the chairperson for the Council of Economic Advisors (CEA), and Alan Blinder, an economics professor from Princeton, was her deputy.[145]

THE CLINTON ECONOMIC AGENDA

Prior to his inauguration, President-elect Clinton met with Federal Reserve Chairman Alan Greenspan in Little Rock, Arkansas. Clinton and Greenspan discussed history and economics, including the Federal Reserve. Greenspan's message to Clinton was that the biggest threat to his presidency would be the budget deficit. He said it contributed to inflation expectations and was the cause of stubbornly high long-term interest rates. Interest rates for 30-year mortgages were then running at over 7%, while short-term interest rates controlled by the Fed were at 3%. Historically, the difference between short-term interest rates (30-, 60-, and 90-day terms) versus long-term interest rates (10-, 20-, and 30-year terms) in the "yield curve" is much closer, on the order of one percentage point. Greenspan told Clinton that if he could provide credible evidence of a serious effort at deficit reduction, then bond traders would have less inflation anxiety and long-term interest rates would come down. The benefits of lower long-term interest rates, Greenspan continued, would be an expanding economy due to consumer spending, a higher stock market, and lower unemployment. After this discussion, deficit reduction became central to President Clinton's economic agenda.[146]

This agenda began to take shape at a meeting of his economic and policy advisors on Thursday, January 7, 1993, in Little Rock, Arkansas. This is where the initial presentations on the different topics were discussed. They talked about deficit reduction and its long-range benefits and short-term costs; the impacts on employment, job creation, and GDP; tax increases for consumption spending (including an energy tax); and a delay to the cost of living adjustments (COLA) for Social Security benefits. They conferred on a short-term stimulus package and health care reform. Finally, they discussed their approach to selling the plan to Congress and the importance of getting legislative approval. After the inauguration, they agreed to President Clinton's goal of providing a detailed plan to Congress and the public by early February.[147]

Although the Democrats controlled the House of Representatives, with a 258 to 177 majority, and they even had a majority in the Senate of 56 to 44, getting President Clinton's budget passed was no easy feat. Not a single Republican voted in favor of his budget. It eventually passed the House on a 219 to 213 vote, and it passed the Senate only with a tie-breaking vote by Vice President Al Gore. The budget had $255 billion in spending cuts and $241 billion in tax increases. It paved the way for stability and predictability in the bond market because it addressed the budget deficit. With inflationary pressures eased, long-term interest rates came down, which provided consumers and businesses with lower borrowing costs. Lower borrowing costs made lower mortgage and auto loan payments possible, which led to more consumer spending because of higher disposable income. Increased consumer spending resulted in a more robust economy, which also led to increased profits, higher valuations, and a higher stock market.[148]

THE NORTH AMERICAN FREE TRADE AGREEMENT

President Clinton pushed the North American Free Trade Agreement (NAFTA) through Congress in his first term. It became effective on January 1, 1994. NAFTA was actually an initiative of his predecessor, President Bush. Free trade – that is, trade that is not encumbered by restrictions, sanctions, or tariffs – is usually beneficial to all countries involved, because it allows the most efficient use of resources and provides the best prices to consumers. During the presidential campaign of 1992, candidate Ross Perot said of NAFTA, "That sucking sound you hear is jobs in the US going to Mexico and Canada." While this was a funny quote, the fact is that both jobs and trade have increased since NAFTA was enacted.[149]

In spite of NAFTA's positive trade and employment effects, a significant Mexican peso crisis occurred soon afterward, and extreme measures were taken to help resolve that situation. The 1994–1995 peso crisis came as a result of the Mexican government's announcement that it would devalue its currency on December 20, 1994. The financial community was caught by surprise and reacted negatively. In the next few days, the Mexican government was forced to float the peso's exchange rate relative to other currencies, and its value dropped precipitously. The US Treasury lent Mexico $12.5 billion from its Exchange Stabilization Fund at the end of January 1995, and that helped resolve the crisis. In addition, the interest rate on that loan was so high that Mexico paid it off early and in full.[150]

OTHER SIGNIFICANT ECONOMIC EVENTS

There were two other significant economic events in the 1990s: the Asian Tiger crisis in 1997 and Long Term Capital Management debacle. The US government had a significant role in dealing with these events. The Asian Tiger crisis evolved from the rapid expansion of Southeast Asian countries, particularly South Korea, Singapore, Malaysia, and Thailand, and their inability to handle the eventual inflation and currency devaluation in their overheated economies. The crux of the issue in the Asian markets was the linking of their currencies to the US dollar at a fixed exchange rate. This attracted investors who supplied the necessary capital for growth and enjoyed the higher interest rates the Asian Tigers provided, along with the exchange rate protection that these countries promised. It was a deal that was too good to be true. As the professional investors who knew better started pulling their money out at the promised exchange rate, these countries started running out of dollars to pay their loans back, and a classic "bank run" ensued. The United States government and the International Monetary Fund (IMF) eventually had to step in to help resolve all these economic issues.[151]

Long Term Capital Management (LTCM) was a hedge fund founded in 1994 that was extremely successful in making money for its clients. Its partnership included several experienced Wall Street traders and two Nobel Prize winners in economics. LTCM practically invented the hedge fund and successfully arbitraged markets to make billions of dollars in profits. And then it overreached and almost toppled the entire financial system. On August 17, 1998, Russia devalued its currency, the ruble, and declared a debt moratorium. In essence, Russia defaulted on its loans, and that default took down almost the entire emerging-economies credit market. After the Russian default, investors fled almost all foreign credit markets for the safety of US Treasuries. LTCM was not only exposed to the Russian default but it also had significant positions in Brazil, which were being affected by the flight from risk toward liquidity.[152]

LTCM's preferred investment was bonds, and the firm was at risk for about $1.8 billion in Russian bonds. The problem was not the $1.8 billion but the network of banks and investment institutions that LTCM owed money to. In addition, its loans were constructed in a way that if it defaulted to one bank, it would default to all the banks it owed. Finally, the size of the LTCM potential loss was magnified by the enormous leverage they employed to amplify their returns. This amplification also worked in reverse, so that in their reversal of fortune, they were at risk of losing tens of billions of dollars. Sixteen companies were on the hook for capital losses of $20 billion, if LTCM were allowed to fail. The CEOs and senior executives of those companies met with Fed representatives to discuss potential solutions of the issue. They agreed to put up almost $4 billion to take over the company and keep it solvent. It was a very unexpected and surprising end for a firm that inspired a great deal of admiration and awe in the financial services industry.[153]

OTHER ECONOMIC EXPANSION EXAMPLES

The era in modern economic history that can come closest to The Great Expansion is the Roaring '20s. Those were the years leading up to the crash of 1929 and the Great Depression. It was a time when everything seemed possible. It was a time when people thought everyone should be rich. Is it a coincidence that both of these examples occurred when the stock market was shooting up like a rocket? On second thought, instead of calling it "The Great Expansion" – how about calling it "The Booming '90s?"

The Roaring '20s was a time of extravagance and excess. World War I was an unpleasant memory, and World War II had yet to unfold. It was a period when America was enjoying its first successes on the international stage, having survived the war with little impact to the country's resources and becoming recognized as a financial leader. During the financial crisis of 1914, US Treasury Secretary and first Federal Reserve Board chairman William G. McAdoo had kept the dollar fixed to gold and successfully ensconced gold as the international money standard.[154] This allowed the US currency to be seen as a legitimate alternative to the British pound and increased the global view of America as a financially sound and stable trading partner.

Other periods of expansion have occurred in recent history, as in the 1950s and the 1960s, but both of those eras were during periods of internal and external strife. The Korean War lasted from 1950 to 1953, and the Vietnam War started when President Kennedy sent troops as military advisors in 1963 and then expanded under President Johnson to a full-fledged war. Also, the internal strife of the civil rights movement continued throughout the 1960s. Both of these expansionary periods enjoyed relatively low inflation and low unemployment. It wasn't until the 1970s that the term "stagflation" was coined. Stagflation was a mash-up of two words: "stagnation" (for a stagnant economy) and "inflation." At that time, inflation was rampant, and the country was experiencing low growth. Ever since that era, executive administrations in the White House have been wary of creating similar scenarios.

The 1980s also gave birth to a new term: Reaganomics. This term was applied to the supply-side economic policies of President Ronald Reagan. He cut taxes and provided economic stimulus through increased defense spending. The intent was to deregulate and allow businesses to thrive, thus increasing tax revenue through greater economic activity. The effects and benefits of Reaganomics are still argued today. Some say the tax cuts and regulatory changes in the 1980s set up the 1990s to enjoy the long expansion of that time period. Others say Reaganomics caused the structural budgetary issues that President Clinton had to address with his deficit reduction package. In any case, one can't argue with the fact that the national budget deficit tripled during President Reagan's two terms in office.

Looking back on the 1990s and comparing it to the other business expansion periods that I have experienced in my life, I would have to conclude that, to me, the 1990s "felt like" the most economically progressive and positive that I can remember. I'm not old enough to know what the 1950s were like, nor do I remember what the 1960s were like, but looking back on my experience from the 1970s, 1980s, and 2000s, those expansions don't seem as powerful. In particular, this decade's recovery from the 2008 financial crisis seems weak and prolonged, and The Great Recession that followed that crisis is a perfect example of the downward phase of the business cycle – recession.

Chapter 14.
The Great Recession

Recessions represent the downward phase of the business cycle. They currently occur about every nine years. I realize that, to economists, this statement is blasphemy. They will tell you that nobody can predict when the next recession will occur. And to some extent, they have a point. No predictions are exact, and there is variability in every cycle. However, it is a useful rule to keep in mind, and one that I have personally followed. I predicted the 2009 recession, based on the recessions from prior years in 2000, 1991, 1982, and 1973. Please note that I do realize the official GDP data from the Federal Reserve website shows that the '70s recession didn't begin until 1974 (as determined by consecutive quarters of negative GDP growth), but from my own personal experience, I consider 1973 to be the start, because my dad was laid off that year due to the economy and was not able to find a job. Similarly, 2001 was the official start of the recession of the 2000s, but based on my own experience, I found the post-dot.com era to be particularly challenging, as I had a difficult time finding a job that year. Based on this trend, I would predict the next recession to occur in 2018.

The Great Recession of 2007–2009 occurred because of the catastrophic failure or near-failure of several financial institutions, including Bear Stearns, Countrywide Financial, Washington Mutual, AIG, Lehman Brothers, Fannie Mae, and Freddie Mac. These epic disasters were brought on by the housing bubble crisis and derivatives. Prior recessions were also precipitated by other significant economic events. These topics were previously discussed in the section on real estate. However, it is interesting to note the timeline and the interaction between the financial institution failures and the Fed's and Treasury's responses to these failures.

The housing market bubble that burst in 2006 clearly sowed the seeds of the financial crisis that occurred in 2008. The first inkling of financial worries started in August 2007, with a crisis in European banks. A liquidity crunch started when France's largest bank, BNP Paribas, stopped redemptions in three of its investment funds that held mortgage-backed securities. This led to tightened credit, as the European banks stopped lending to each other. The European Central Bank stepped in to provide liquidity to the market. Another European banking crisis occurred in September 2007, when Northern Rock, the fifth largest bank in the United Kingdom, requested and received emergency support from the Bank of England. This was reported by the BBC, and by the next morning long lines formed around every branch of the "Rock." It was a shocking sight on television screens across the island nation. "In one day, Northern Rock depositors withdrew £1 billion in the first run on a British bank since Overend, Gurney and Company collapsed in 1866, some 141 years before."[155]

BEAR STEARNS STARTS A DOMINO EFFECT

Then in March 2008, the Bear Stearns crisis started. Bear Stearns was the smallest of the five major investment banks on Wall Street. In the first week of March, their stock fell almost 20%, and it was under intense pressure to fall further. Bear Stearns was heavily invested in collateralized debt obligations (CDOs), and these investments would doom the company. The second week of March 2008 saw Bear Stearns's stock price drop another 50%. Liquidity issues were hammering the firm, as other banks and financial institutions traded out of positions with Bear Stearns. It was similar to a bank run, in which nobody wanted to be the last person to the cashier window to ask for their money, only to be told there wasn't any left. Bear Stearns burned through almost $10 billion in withdrawals in a week, and they were running low on cash reserves. Whatever move they were going to make, they had to make soon, or they would be bankrupt. Timothy Geithner, President of the Federal Reserve

Bank of New York, and Ben Bernanke, Chairman of the Federal Reserve, were closely monitoring the situation and decided quick action was required. They lined up a buyer – Jamie Dimon, CEO of JP Morgan Chase – and agreed to guarantee a $30 billion loan to cover Bear's toxic mortgage assets. Dimon negotiated a deal for Bear Stearns at $2 per share, or about $250 million. However, when the JP Morgan lawyers reviewed the deal arraigned by the government, it was considerably riskier than originally thought. JP Morgan renegotiated the deal and eventually bought Bear Stearns for $10 per share.[156]

By mid-2008, Fannie Mae and Freddie Mac were struggling. In the first two weeks of July, both Fannie and Freddie lost half their stock value, reflecting the market's legitimate concerns about these government-sponsored entities' (GSEs) ability to withstand the housing market crash. Lehman Brothers had speculated that the GSEs might require up to $75 billion in additional capital. Lehman undershot by a significant amount. The government eventually put up $100 billion for each GSE to ensure adequate capital was available. It took a significant Congressional and Treasury effort to provide funding and policy changes that allowed that bailout to happen, but with the Housing and Economic Recovery Act (HERA) legislation passing the Senate on July 26, these necessary changes could occur. Then, in September 2008, they were both taken over by the government for over $100 billion each (as compared to the $1.2 billion JP Morgan paid for Bear Stearns). By the time the Obama administration took office in January 2009, those numbers had actually doubled to $200 billion for each GSE.[157]

The wheels started coming off in late September, as Lehman Brothers went bankrupt after many attempts to find a buyer or merger opportunity. Prospective suitors included the Korean Development Bank, Bank of America, and Barclays. Richard Fuld, CEO and chairman of Lehman Brothers, stared bankruptcy in the face and blinked. A last-minute Hail Mary attempt to sell Lehman to Barclays was held up by protocol requiring a vote by Barclays's shareholders – which the British government refused to waive. Some in the financial community blame the British government for Lehman Brothers' failure. Still others blame the US government's refusal to save the company from going under for Lehman's failure and the subsequent market panic and Wall Street meltdown.[158]

In addition, AIG – an insurer of mortgage-backed securities – failed and was bailed out by the same government entities that would not save Lehman. The credit markets ground to a halt, and there was panic on Wall Street. The Fed funneled $85 billion to AIG. Bank of America bought Merrill Lynch for $50 billion, JP Morgan purchased Washington Mutual for $1.9 billion, and Wells Fargo acquired Wachovia for $15.4 billion. From March 2008 to September 2008, no less than nine major financial institutions were acquired, bailed out, or went bankrupt: Bear Stearns, IndyMac Bank, Fannie Mae, Freddie Mac, Lehman Brothers, AIG, Merrill Lynch, Washington Mutual, and Wachovia. In an already consolidated industry with many firms that were "too big to fail," the liquidations and mergers only brought more consolidation and even bigger firms.[159]

BERNANKE AND PAULSON DEVISE A PLAN

On September 18, 2008, Fed Chairman Bernanke and Treasury Secretary Paulson went to the president to devise a plan to keep Wall Street from having a complete financial meltdown. Eventually, they came up with the Troubled Asset Relief Program (TARP) to provide up to $700 billion to purchase toxic assets from the financial markets. Then they had to go to Congress to get approval for their plan. Legislators wanted to limit the amount of funding for TARP to $200 billion, but eventually they accepted a TARP bill that amounted to a line of credit of $700 billion for the Treasury. The House of Representatives rejected the bill on Monday, September 29, by a vote of 228 to 205. On October 1, the Senate approved TARP by 74 to 25. On a second try on October 3, the House agreed to TARP by a vote of 263 to 171.[160]

The financial crisis started a domino effect of layoffs, corporation restructurings, downsizing, and bankruptcies. At that time, almost half the employees in the country were in the financial services industry or real estate. At one point, it seemed like everybody was involved in real estate or the mortgage industry. Everyone seemed to be selling everyone else property or a better refinance rate. As banks failed and merged, a significant proportion of these employees soon became unemployed. And the many peripheral organizations and companies that supported these industries also lost their clientele and source funding to continue operations. This significant increase in unemployment created a severe drag on the economy.

By October 2009, unemployment hit 10%, and many companies were just beginning to feel the impact. As the real estate market went into a tailspin, the values of homes from California to New York fell by 30% or more. Then, as home asset values turned upside down, with a significant portion of mortgages exceeding the values of the properties financed, many people simply walked away. This was depicted in film when actor Tom Hanks walked away from his home in the movie *Larry Crowne*. His character told his banker that he could no longer afford his home, so he was transferring the debt back to the bank.[161] This was a case of art reflecting life, and that reflection occurred many times over. The number of foreclosed homes across the country skyrocketed, as people were laid off due to the economy or were forced into higher payments when their adjustable-rate mortgages adjusted to a higher value. Others who had bought their homes with "teaser" rates soon found out they could not afford those homes when the rates became based on the nominal London Interbank Overnight Rate (LIBOR).

The financial crisis also affected businesses across the country, not just the banking and real estate businesses. The credit crunch impacted all firms. Another example of the stress the recession caused was the bailout of the automobile companies General Motors and Chrysler. The federal government provided loan guarantees and other financial aid to these manufacturers because they were threatened by overseas competition and the restrictions the credit crunch put on new and used car loans. They were also impacted when significant numbers of people put off these major purchases due to the instability in the economy. These and the other massive corporate failures are the reasons the Great Recession is one of the worst on record.

OTHER ECONOMIC RECESSION EXAMPLES

Before the Great Recession was the recession of 2000, caused by the collapse of the stock market and the end of the dot-com boom in the run-up to Y2K. With the end of so many financial gains that had made instant stock millionaires from tech IPOs and the rampant speculation on Internet stocks, the sudden removal of that power source to the economy caused an instantaneous cooling and slowdown in a broad spectrum of spending. With less spending and less taxes reaped from the IPOs, the overall economy suffered and eventually took down the Democratic Party's rule of the White House.

NBER statistics officially state that the recession prior to the Great Recession occurred in 2001. I think that is a reflection of the momentum effect from the productivity gains in the 1990s, which pushed forward into the 2000s and allowed companies to maintain economic profit and production. Personally, I had received my MBA from UC Irvine in 1999 and was looking to change companies in 2000, because the plant I was working at was being shut down and the work was moving to Palmdale or Oklahoma City. After the dot-com bust and stock market crash, I found it extremely difficult to land a new job. This is why I feel that the recession unofficially started in 2000.

The end of the Cold War caused the recession of 1991. As soon as the Berlin Wall came down in November 1989, the US government shifted priorities and started spending less on defense. This was equivalent to taking your foot off the gas pedal in an automobile on the freeway. What happened afterward was a domino effect of momentum away from spending and a true impact to incomes and employment (with all its associated trickle-down effects), to the point where companies were being shut down and an aerospace merger mania ensued.

The recession in 1982 was caused by Fed Chairman Volcker raising interest rates to extreme levels to squeeze inflation out of the economy. He was extremely effective in his efforts; however, the result of raising interest rates and choking off the money supply was a severe recession. The unemployment level reached as high as 10.8%, and the country suffered multiple economic challenges. Many people struggled, and there were many publicized strikes. One such strike was the air traffic control-lers (ATC) strike. Because the ATC union was a government employee union, President Reagan decided he would not allow government work-ers to shut down a critical transportation service and cripple an already badly damaged economy. So, he ordered them back to work, and when they refused, he fired them.

The 1973–1974 recession, caused by the OPEC oil embargo, was also extremely harsh. The oil embargo set off a chain of events, starting with a decline in production and manufacturing due to the lack of oil and the shock of high oil prices. The cut in production affected staffing, because less personnel were required to produce the number of products to meet demand, so many workers were laid off. The cumulative national effect of high production prices and low profits squeezed companies to further streamline operations and/or further reduce staff. Then people started purchasing less, due to the decreased purchasing power of their salaries and the lower levels of inventory and products on the shelves.

In prior decades going back to the early 1900s, recessions were much more severe, and there were more frequent boom-and-bust cycles. Many of these cycles were related to the stock market and the interplay be-tween credit and liquidity in the market, with the speculation and bub-bles that occur when easy money is available – the relationship between greed and fear. However, since the 1960s and the application of modern macroeconomics – especially the lessons from John Maynard Keynes and Keynesian economics – the trend has been toward less frequent and less severe recessions.

The difference between a recession and a depression is the severity of the economic situation. Or, as that famous cowboy and comedian Will Rogers used to say, "It's a recession if your neighbor loses his job; it's a depression if you lose yours." Keynesian economics was developed as a means of getting out of the 1930s Depression. President Franklin D. Roo-sevelt used Keynesian economics as the basis for his strategy to get the United States moving again after the debacle of the Hoover era and the disastrous policies of that administration. The lessons learned from Keynes were that, in order to facilitate the workings of the natural sales

and purchases of goods and services, there needed to be a lubricant applied whenever things got stuck – as in the 1930s Depression. He said
the government needed to come in and apply policies relating to the
availability of credit, liquidity, and employment that would aid in a return to normal economic conditions.

FORECASTING ECONOMIC RECESSIONS

In March 2006, I attended a book launch for *The Well-Timed Strategy:
Managing the Business Cycle for Competitive Advantage*, written by my
macroeconomics professor, Dr. Peter Navarro. During the question and
answer session, I asked him if we should expect a recession in 2009. He
stated that recessions were difficult to predict and went on to the next
question. Economists are typically reticent to forecast recessions. Even
after a recession occurs, they will argue over when it started and how
long it lasted, and this subject is almost its own field in the industry.

The fact that recessions are difficult to predict shouldn't keep us from
trying to anticipate their arrival. If you know a recession is coming, you
can prepare for the storm, much as people prepare for a hurricane in the
Southeast or a tornado in the Midwest. You just have to know what to
look for and have a plan or strategy prepared to move quickly if the
economy goes south. In fact, predicting the economy is a bit like predicting the weather: In general, you can be correct about what will happen,
but unexpected events can and do occur.

If world events and other convergences conspire to maintain the cyclical nine-year pattern of recessions, then the next recession should occur in 2018. I believe there will be a worldwide shortage of natural
resources in the coming years, due to the overproduction of products
that use these sources of natural materials. The Chinese are aware of this
coming shortage, and according to economist Dambisa Moyo's book
*Winner Take All: China's Race for Resources and What It Means for the
World*, they are preparing for the worst and doing what they can to lock
up their supply of critical food, fuel, and water supplies for the coming
crisis.[162]

These restrictions of natural resources will cause a never-ending spiral of inflation, as different countries start hoarding or buying larger and larger amounts of oil, property, and gold. In all likelihood, this will be driven by the increasing capitalization of the Chinese market and the growing appetites of Chinese consumers. Once 1.3 billion Chinese get a taste of the good life, there will be no going back. Demand will drive prices in a long-term upward trend that will cause major changes in the structure of the world economy. Other developing countries, such as India, Brazil, countries in Southeast Asia, and countries on the African continent, are also producing more middle-class citizens, who will add to the pressure on product prices.

Our current economy is based on an oil and gas energy system. This is like a house of cards that will eventually fall down and crumble. Our economy is built over a sinkhole that is comprised of the remains of hundreds of thousands of fossils from millions of years ago. There is only so much oil, and eventually it will run out. But it doesn't even have to run out for there to be a huge impact on our society and economy. An oil crisis could cause a major shift in the structure of our economy. As prices rise due to the supply/demand curve, every product across the spectrum of goods and services will have to increase in order to maintain equilibrium.

Chapter 15.
The Juglar Business Cycle

Joseph Schumpeter, who defined the length and phases of the business cycle in his classic 1939 book *Business Cycles*, stated that there are definite investment cycles that correspond to the four stages of a sinusoidal wave. These four stages constitute the typical nine-year business cycle, which has been shown to exist with "considerable regularity." Joseph Schumpeter called these nine-year periods "Juglar cycles," for Clement Juglar, who was the first to interpret the changes in interest rates, prices, and banking data as proof of the existence of an underlying wave or cycle. "His great merit is that he pushed the crisis into the background and that he discovered below it another, much more fundamental, phenomenon."[163] Schumpeter also states that the nine-year Juglar cycle is composed of a multiple of Kitchin cycles.

Schumpeter used work published by the statistician Joseph Kitchin to correlate the stages of the business cycle to a definite time phase, and that is why the nine-year business cycle is a multiple of the Kitchin cycle. Kitchin showed that there are approximately three phases of development or investment that successively operate to form a fully sinusoidal cycle that represents the natural harmonics of business. Each phase of the Kitchin cycle appears to be about three years long. This means that each Juglar cycle is comprised of three Kitchin cycles. Schumpeter also noted that the Kondratieff cycle is composed of six Juglar cycles (of about nine years each) for a total of about 54 years. He expanded on that work to explain why the cycle exists and why it is repeatable. He also emphasized that when the peaks or troughs of these different cycles synchronize, the effect is amplified to make things much better – or worse: "...the coincidence at any time of corresponding phases of all three cycles will always produce phenomena of unusual intensity, especially if the phases that coincide are those of prosperity or depression."[164]

THE KONDRATIEFF LONG WAVE

Schumpeter found that the Juglar business cycle is made up of three consecutive Kitchin cycles, each of which represents a different component with respect to an innovation that's created, the consumer response to that new product, and the competition from other entities trying to receive their share of the profits available to the entrepreneurs who first created the product. The innovation, like a stone dropped into a calm body of water, sends out multiple waves. The first wave comes from the introduction of the new product. The second wave is associated with competitors' responses to the new innovation. And the third wave results from the absorption of the two prior waves into the overall economic activity occurring at that time. These three Kitchin cycles constitute the overall Juglar cycle, and six of these Juglar cycles of nine years each make up the overall Kondratieff Long Wave (see Figure 19).[165]

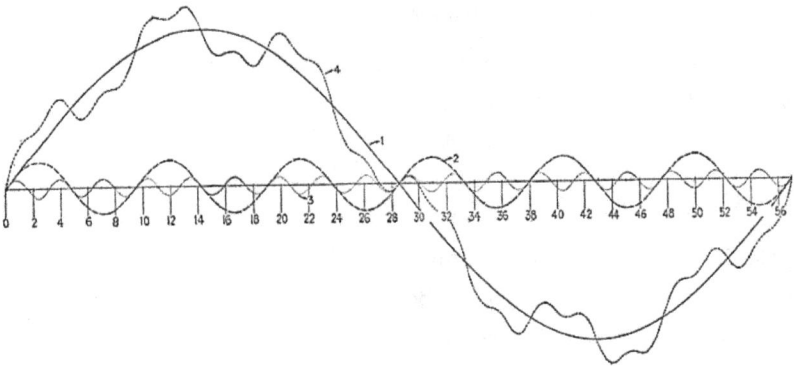

Figure 19. Kondratieff (1), Juglar (2), and Kitchin (3) Cycles, per Schumpeter[166]

The Long Wave represents major movements in the economic profile and history surrounding and/or driving each of the major waves. The Long Wave associated with the cycle during the Great Depression occurred from 1897 to1951 and is known as the "age of electricity" cycle. The cycle that has just ended, from 1952 to 2006, started during the Cold War era and ended with the Iraq and Afghanistan wars. I call this the "age of information technology" cycle, as its underlying innovation was the invention of the Shockley transistor and the silicon microchip. The cycle we are in now has already started and should last from 2007 to about 2060. I would expect it to be a significant era of change and discontinuity. It remains to be seen what innovation will be the driver for this cycle, but I have predicted in the section on inflation that it will be associated with energy. The reason that is a prediction, as opposed to a statement, is because, even though those inventions that are the cause of the current Long Wave cycle already exist, it takes time and a historical perspective to identify the event or invention that starts it all.

INNOVATION DRIVES THE BUSINESS CYCLE

Schumpeter stated that the business cycle starts with the entrepreneur having an idea and innovating a new way to build, implement, or solve something. "Motivation is supplied by the prospect of profit."[167] As the entrepreneur spends savings to create the new widget, this upsets the equilibrium of the system and causes the economy to expand. The prior state of the economy had no unemployed resources, thus wages and/or costs of production will rise, which will cause older firms to reinvest in the company or product. Then competition will create additional demand for material or labor. This eventually leads other firms to join in and plan for additional production, eventually resulting in overinvestment and unrealistic projections of sales and profit. When sales disappoint, production is cut and employment is reduced, thereby reducing GDP growth and slowing the economy.[168]

Depending on how quickly the economy expands and how overheated the response is to that prior innovation, the recession could lead to a depression or a crisis of some proportion. The business cycle could now zip right past the equilibrium line and into negative territory, as crisis turns to disaster and conditions worsen. Unemployment will rise as the firms that over expanded, expecting significant growth, find that their capital outlay will incur negative returns, and so they must cut labor re-sources to remain profitable and cost competitive. As unemployment worsens, economic activity across the board is reduced, as employees seek to minimize their spending to preserve their savings. As for the business enterprise, reorganization and adaptation remain the key tools to confront and respond to the crisis. Recovery will only occur once the elimination of excess capacity in plant, personnel, and equipment is real-ized. The curve of the business cycle will move back toward equilibrium and the neutral state, until the next big idea causes another wave of in-novation and creative destruction.[169]

Because the innovation for the current Long Wave forms the basis of the long-term prospects for that 54-year period, you can use these stages like the hands of a giant clock, so you can tell what economic time it is. If you are early in the cycle, then the current latest invention (steam pow-er, electricity, or the silicon transistor) will provide lots of opportunity for economic growth and profit. If you are in the middle of the cycle, em-ployment is growing, money is flowing, and good times are rolling. At the end of the cycle, dark clouds arrive and remain overhead, unemployment rises, and people start to feel a certain discontent. Then comes the be-ginning of the next cycle, which builds upon the previous one and pro-vides new innovations and new opportunities for growth. "The start of a new trend in our economy cannot be forecast, as we have seen. But even without expecting any lift in the trend lines, this new long-term cycle could be read in advance to provide hope for a coming long-term era of prosperity and progress in our nation, regardless of any depression that may intervene."[170]

Without Schumpeter's work, economics truly would be a "dismal sci-ence." Economics got that nickname because one of its early practition-ers, Thomas Robert Malthus, had predicted that there would be a worldwide food crisis, based on population growth and the food supply's inability to keep up. This prediction did not come true because of tech-nology and the advancement of farming techniques and machinery. In-novation, driven by the capitalistic desire for monetary reward – the "motivation" ascribed by Schumpeter – creates wave after wave of new ideas and new technology – what Schumpeter called "innovation" – to confront and resolve the issues and needs faced by the human race. Schumpeter is also credited with coining the phrase "creative destruction" in his book *Capitalism, Socialism, and Democracy*, published in 1942. In that book, Schumpeter furthered his ideas on innovation as the driving force in economic growth and on the evolutionary changes to businesses wrought by those innovations.

THE BUSINESS CYCLE PROVIDES A HEARTBEAT

Schumpeter's work is referenced in Dewey and Dakin's *Cycles: The Science of Prediction* for both the nine-year business cycle and the 54-year Kondratieff Long Wave. Dewey and Dakin use Schumpeter's data and figures to show how the 54-year Long Wave is a worldwide phenomenon. Commodity and wholesale prices in Germany, the United Kingdom, and the United States follow the same curve, with the same 54-year period, and that "…every Kondratieff cycle has been uniquely characterized by some particularly important economic or industrial innovation."[171] They go on to say that as prices come down, unemployment goes up, as employers try to maintain profits by reducing labor expenses. This is a traditional and expected first response by management. "For, as prices decline, manufacturers naturally look for ways to eliminate extra man-hours, to turn out their product for less."[172]

Dewey and Dakin also reference Schumpeter's work in their analysis and confirmation of the nine-year business cycle. They discuss Schumpeter's use of the Juglar cycle in his book on business cycles and note the argument that there is not a single wave (or cycle) in effect here, but the interference of several waves or cycles of different periodicities or wavelengths. Dewey and Dakin go one step further and show how the nine-year business cycle is fundamental to other cycles. They show in Figure 20 that wholesale prices (the 54-year Kondratieff Long Wave) have deviations from the mean that repeat in nine-year patterns.

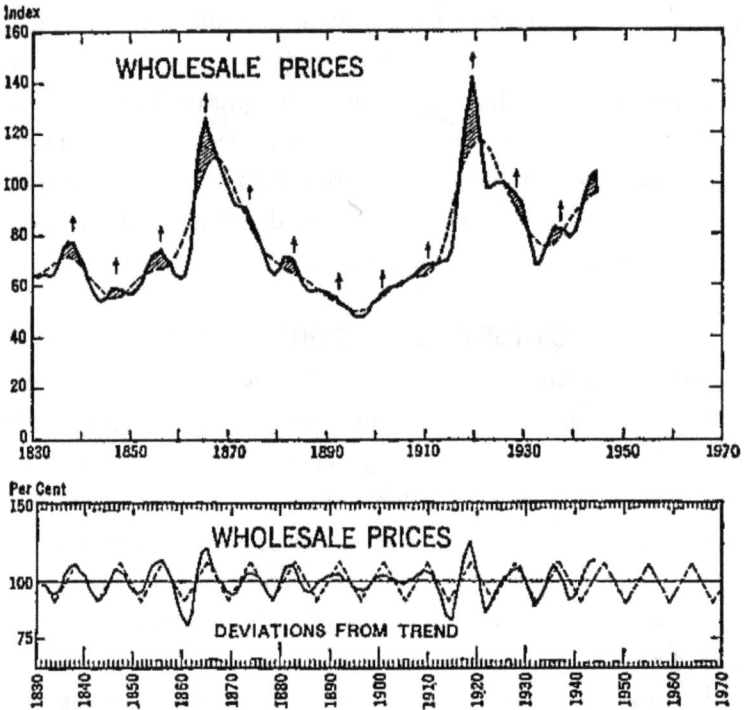

Figure 20. Wholesale Price Deviations (9-year Pattern)[173]

They also show in Figure 21 that common stock prices (the 36-year stock market cycle) have deviations from the mean that repeat in nine-year patterns. This shows the underlying business cycle wave is *fundamental* to both the Long Wave (inflation) and the stock market cycle. "This rhythm of 9 years, which is of such importance in our economic statistics, is like every other rhythm we discuss here – it is the registering of *a wave of activity in the economic organism*."[174]

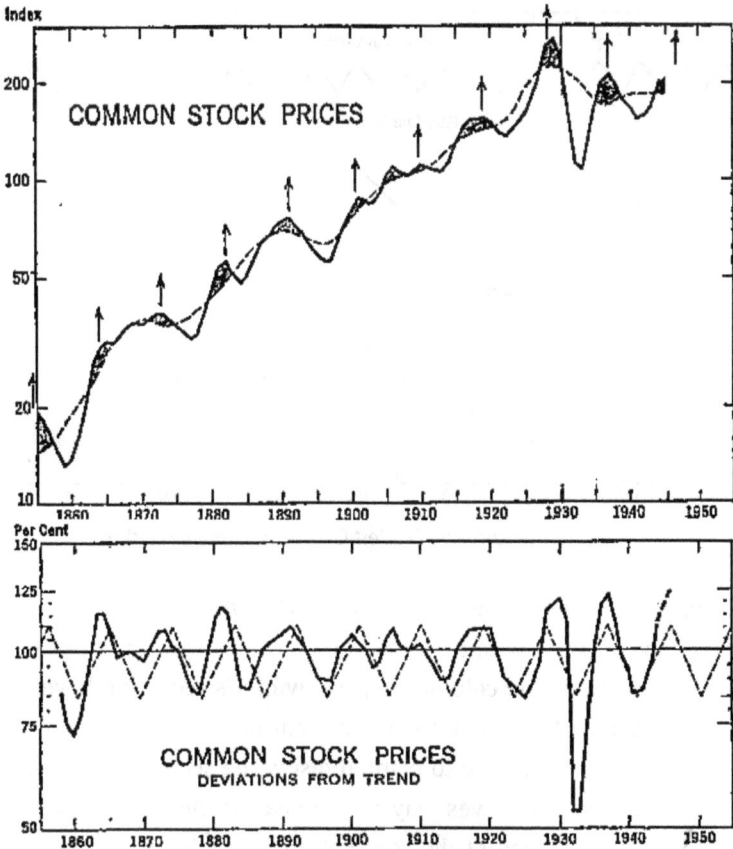

Figure 21. Common Stock Price Deviations (9-year Pattern)[175]

Both the Dewey and Dakin model and the Schumpeter model show multiple simultaneous cycles operating in their respective methodologies. Dewey and Dakin show the nine-year business cycle combined with the 54-year Long Wave and the net effect (see Figure 22).[176] Schumpeter's model combines the Kitchin 40-month cycle with the Juglar nine-year cycle and the Kondratieff 54-year cycle. These models both reflect more accurately the heuristically determined prices and provide a method for predicting future performance.[177]

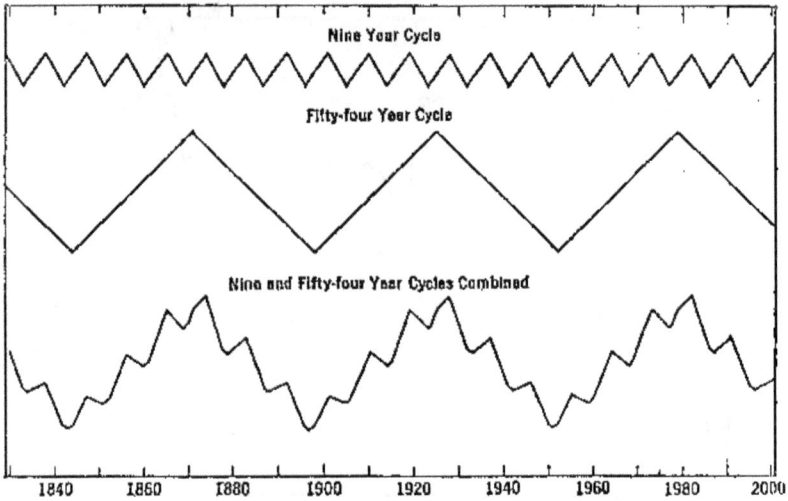

Figure 22. Juglar and Kondratieff Cycles, per Dewey and Dakin

As already explained, the business cycle mimics the seasons of the year. The cycle starts with a spring-like recovery from the prior cycle's recession. The frost and cold of the prior winter's recession have faded, and the air is now filled with the fresh scent of newness. The ground is wet with dew, and it is time to plant and sow the seeds of good fortune. The spring of recovery gives way to the heat of the summer, with the expansion and optimism of the renewal finally taking hold, and people and decision makers interpret the improving climate as the opportunity to invest and seek higher returns – the chance to increase sales and profits.

The heat of the summer expansion eventually gives way to overexpansion and overconfidence in the economy, which leads to bad decision making. As this unrealistic expectation in continued and possibly exponential expansion continues, it reaches a breaking point, which causes the next crisis phase. The crisis of autumn leads to the winter of recession, and everything slows down, almost to a halt. The recession causes the flow of capital, goods, and services to freeze up. This starts a chain reaction as businesses respond to the new economic reality. Each decision made by business leaders impacts some aspect of the overall economy.

KEYNES BUSINESS CYCLE THEORY

John Maynard Keynes was a believer in the existence of business cycles and stated in his classic treatise *The General Theory of Employment, Interest, and Money*: "It is upon the fact that fluctuations tend to wear themselves out before proceeding to extremes and eventually reversing themselves, that the theory of business cycles having a regular phase has been founded." He also said that prices behave in a similar way in that, after some price disturbance, there will be a level at which they will become relatively stable.[178]

Keynes discusses in a separate chapter of *The General Theory* the industrial trade cycle, in which he recognizes the cyclical nature of business where "...there is some recognizable degree of regularity in the time-sequence and duration of the upward and downward movements."[179] He goes on to explain that the time component of the trade cycle is logically due to the actions and reactions of the individual participants in the equation. There are inventories of durable goods that have to be liquidated before new stock is bought, there is the time lag of new products and newly produced goods, and there are decisions that are made by the entrepreneurs and business leaders to invest or react to economic conditions. These all combine to provide the net effect on the system of a rise in "...the upward direction, the forces propelling it upward at first gather force and have a cumulative effect on one another but gradually lose their strength, until at a certain point they tend to be replaced by forces operating in the opposite direction; which in turn gather force for a time and accentuate one another, until they, too, having reached their maximum development, wane, and give place to their opposite."[180]

TOOLS FOR ECONOMIC FORECASTING

Tools and techniques are available to help predict when the next recession or the next expansion may occur. The first tool is the yield curve.

The yield curve shows the difference (or the spread, in basis points) between the short-term and long-term rates on US Treasury securities. If the short-term rates are lower in the curve than the long-term rates by 100 to 200 basis points, then this is a "normal" curve, and the economy is healthy. If the yield curve is "inverted" – that is, if the short-term rates are higher than the long-term rates – then the economy is primed for a recession. If the yield curve has a "steep" difference between short- and long-term rates (more than 200 basis points), then a significant business expansion is around the corner.[181]

The second tool to use in predicting the next recession is the stock market. The stock market always leads the economic business cycle by three to six months. The third and fourth tools are the Conference Board's Index of Leading Economic Indicators (LEI) and the Economic Cycle Research Institute (ECRI) dashboard. The LEI is heavily weighted by the yield curve and stock prices. The ECRI dashboard includes both the Weekly Leading Index (a subset of the LEI) and the Future Inflation Gauge (FIG). Clients of these firms privately obtain both these tools for an unspecified price. The fifth and final tool to determine the imminence of the next recession is the price of oil. Sharp increases in the price of oil tend to immediately impact the economy and start a chain reaction that ends with the start of the next recession.[182]

The question is not whether or not the business cycle exists, but rather, what is the length and periodicity of this cycle? Definitions and debates abound regarding the length of the business cycle and its predictability. As I've stated in this section, there is plenty of topical material regarding the business cycle. There are also plenty of models and predictions for where we are on the cycle and when the next recession will be. The point is not to get caught up in the specifics and details of the current cycle, but to step back and look at the forest – not the trees – to get the big picture of what is going on and how that can help you with your decision making. You should also think about how the other cycles interact with each other, and account for the multiplier effect if the other cycles are in or out of phase with each other. Using the approach in the next section, you can understand where you are and where you are going in the next few years. With that information, you can make informed decisions that will keep you on track for your goals and maintain your plans for the future.

Chapter 16.
What's Next for Business

At some point in the business cycle, there will be a significant drop in stock market prices. This will be the first clear indication that we are at the end of the expansion part of the cycle and moving toward the recession phase, as the stock market leads the business cycle by about six months. The remaining years of the decade, after the 2016 election, could see sluggish economic growth, as we grind toward the eventual slowdown of the economy. I am predicting a 2018 recession, which will be the culmination of several years of slowing (but not negative) economic growth and the downsizing of companies, as they try to deal with higher costs and lower profits. I also expect that labor as a cost will resurface as the primary target of CEOs and CFOs, and there will be a renewed effort to maximize "non-touch" processes, automation, and artificial intelligence to cut expenses. The only companies that will be able to maintain their profit margins will be those in semi monopolistic positions of competitive advantage or those that are industry leaders with exclusivity.

The Great Recession of 2007–2009 was one of the most severe in history. Will the recession of 2018 be as rough? There are so many potential drivers for the next recession that it is difficult to predict what will push the economy over. Many central banks are propping up their national economies by printing money. This should drive inflation; however, with interest rates at or near zero percent, inflation is a difficult argument to make. Despite that, as you have already read in Section I, I have made that argument. I believe that rising inflation is in our future. The question is, how significant of an impact will it have?

A REVIEW OF THE CURRENT BUSINESS CYCLE

In order to answer that question, I will review the most recent business cycle and then try to project what the next business cycle will look like – from recession to recovery to expansion to crisis. I already discussed the Great Recession of 2009 in great detail, so this recession section will not be very extensive. The Great Recession actually started in 2007 and continued for six consecutive quarters. This was one of the longest periods of negative GDP growth in US history. And the year 2008 averaged negative GDP growth for the entire year – one of the very few years in which this has happened. The year 2010 saw some improvement; however, the unemployment numbers for the year were some of the worst of the past 50 years. The Great Recession was extensive in breadth and depth, and it will be remembered as the worst since the Great Depression.

The recovery phase was long and unpleasant, but at least it is behind us. The Arab Spring started in 2011, with Tunisian president Zine El Abidine Ben Ali fleeing to Saudi Arabia, Egyptian president Hosni Mubarak resigning and leaving control of Egypt in the hands of the military, and Libyan leader Muammar Gaddafi being killed. In an unrelated event, an American raid in Pakistan killed Osama Bin Laden, and President Obama declared an end to the Iraq war. US economic output, in terms of real GDP, was negative in the first quarter of 2011, but it rebounded and was positive the rest of the year, with average growth of just over 2%. Unemployment for the year was 8.9%, better than 2010 by 0.7%.

In 2012, the Large Hadron Collider in CERN announced the empirical existence of the Higgs boson, an elementary particle in quantum electrodynamics (QED); European Union finance ministers agreed to a €130 billion Greek bailout; and the UN Climate Change conference agreed to extend the Kyoto Protocol to the year 2020. The year 2012 also saw steady improvement in the housing sector, as quantitative easing (QE) was implemented by the Fed to reduce long-term interest rates. The QE was successful in lowering long-term rates on the order of 1%–2% on 30-year fixed-rate loans. This begat a flurry of refinancing and also some increased activity in the home construction industry. US economic output in terms of real GDP was positive all year in 2012, with average growth of just under 2%. Unemployment for the year was 8.1%, an improvement over the prior year by 0.8%.

The year 2013 had several significant events, of which I will note only a few. On Patriot's Day, Chechen Islamists planted two bombs at the Boston Marathon, killing three people and injuring 264 others. National Security Agency employee Eric Snowden provided news outlets with details of a mass government surveillance program and then fled to Russia. In fact, the December 18, 2013, Federal Open Market Committee meeting press release stated: "Information received since the Federal Open Market Committee met in October indicates that economic activity is expanding at a moderate pace. Labor market conditions have shown further improvement; the unemployment rate has declined but remains elevated."[183] Real GDP grew quarter over quarter in 2013 until the fourth quarter, with an average growth of 2.2% for the year. Unemployment was 7.4%, an increase of 0.7% over the prior year.

In 2014, the expansion phase of the business cycle saw continued growth and improvement in both the GDP and employment numbers. The December 2013 FOMC meeting also determined to continue the Fed's commitment to ensuring the nation's economic recovery: "Beginning in January, the Committee will add to its holdings of agency mortgage-backed securities at a pace of $35 billion per month rather than $40 billion per month, and will add to its holdings of longer-term Treasury securities at a pace of $40 billion per month rather than $45 billion per month."[184] For the year ending December 31, 2014, the NASDAQ gained close to 15%, unemployment was down to 5.6%, and GDP growth was 2.4%.

As the economy expanded, the Federal Reserve reduced and eventually eliminated its practice of purchasing mortgage-backed securities (MBS) and Treasury securities in 2015. In addition, in December 2015 the Fed increased the Federal Funds Rate for the first time in over six years. I believe the Fed will have to continue to raise interest rates to hold inflation in check. If the current Fed chair, Janet Yellen, does not "take away the punch bowl" soon, then we will certainly be on our way to pushing the inflation pendulum to the other side, toward inflation. The effects of inflation on the business cycle are twofold: Inflation puts pressure on producers to consider price increases in their products and, if prices get too high, it can cause consumers to cut back on spending, leading to a slowdown in consumption and eventually a recession.

FORCES DRIVING THE NEXT BUSINESS CYCLE

Internet giants that led the last economic expansion: Apple, Amazon, Google, and Facebook will play a part in the next expansion. Apple is a leader in innovation, the driving force behind all economic expansions. Apple's technology products have shaped the world in which we live. Amazon has become the Wal-Mart of the Internet: the retailer is the point-of-sale choice for the online masses. Google has continued to be the advertising and search king, providing billions of dollars of revenue to its loyal stockholders. Facebook will eventually turn its one billion users into cash-generating and revenue-streaming units. Google and Facebook seem to be challenging each other for Internet user supremacy.

Facebook is a worldwide phenomenon that has the potential to create significant economic activity. It has already proven to be an effective social force relative to engaging thousands of users, as it did in the Arab Spring of 2011. Facebook was used as a medium for communicating and coordinating demonstrations and gatherings. It has also been used effectively in coordinating flash mob activity throughout the world. The efficacy of Facebook as a tool for social change will be tied to its continued relevance as the tool of choice for the majority of its users. Its ubiquity is currently unequalled; however, as with all technology, this could change. What is popular today may not be popular tomorrow, and its current "coolness" factor could wear off. In fact, it is wearing off with certain segments of the younger population, as they turn to tools and websites that their parents are not aware of. This will be Facebook's greatest challenge in the next few years, as it struggles with size and scope and tries to remain on top as the preferred tool for social media.

What are the possible replacement technologies for Facebook? The key leverage for Facebook is its one billion users – a significant barrier for any competitor to overcome. The future challengers that come on the scene will need to provide equivalent functionality but have additional features that enhance usability and integration into everyday life. It seems that Facebook is currently attempting to maintain its leadership position by purchasing all potential competitors and adding additional functionality through purchases or outright development. This was not the original platform, as Facebook has traditionally allowed users to enhance content via their own creativity. It remains to be seen how this Internet giant will proceed.

OIL, INFLATION, AND THE BUSINESS CYCLE

The crisis years will come with many challenges. Geopolitically, there is the continued extremist activity in the Mideast, with Syria in a continuing civil war, Iraq with its own internal tensions and strife due to the US troop pull-out at the end of 2014, and Iran heightening angst as it attempts to become the next nuclear-capable country, which was somewhat mitigated by the recent US-Iran treaty. As tensions in the Mideast rise, this puts pressure on oil supplies and worldwide oil prices. In addition, China is a rising economic and military power, flexing its muscles in territorial disputes but internally challenged by keeping its citizens on the path to economic prosperity. Furthermore, Russia is embarking on an imperialistic course, as it absorbs Crimea into the motherland and threatens Ukraine with its military advances. Finally, the changing weather patterns caused by global warming are challenging the political stability of several developing countries and significant areas of the world. As famine and disease caused by drought and flooding in different parts of the globe becomes more widespread, more and more countries will be subject to civil unrest.

The demand for oil will drive increases for gas and petroleum-based products. I envision $5-per-gallon gas in our future. Then, when the worldwide production of oil peaks, there will be a chain of events of price changes and increases in expectations of higher prices that will drive inflation. When pump prices double to $10 per gallon, we will see the kind of inflationary effects that the 1973–1974 oil crisis had on the economy. As the price of oil increases, the prices of all other products will follow, because of the transportation costs included in every product. In addition, there are manufacturing costs that also have to be reflected in those products, because the price of electricity and natural gas also will increase.

The effects of inflation on the business cycle are twofold: Inflation causes pressure on producers to consider price increases in their products (which can only occur if they have strong positioning and pricing power), and if prices get too high, it can cause consumers to cut back on spending, causing a slowdown in consumption and possibly a recession. I have already predicted a recession in 2018, and I think the effects of inflation will impact this recession (either directly or indirectly). Inflation will cause a drag on economic activity, and GDP will suffer as a result. I believe that inflation will create a 1%–2% GDP drag on the economy, and inflation expectations could drive consumer behavior.

The end of oil is not the only issue in our future. We also need to consider what the burning of fossil fuels has done to our environment, along with the ecological and economic impacts it has had to date and the additional impacts it will have in the future. Greenhouse gases are higher than they have been in almost a million years. Climate change will cause the oceans to rise, due to the melting of the polar ice caps and the ice pack on Greenland, which is estimated will completely disappear, once the earth's temperature rises 2–7 degrees above the average pre-industrial temperature.[185] Not only are noxious gases increasing in our atmosphere, causing respiratory diseases in millions of people across the planet, but they are also causing acid rain on the oceans and affecting thousands of species of plants and animals.

CLIMATE CHANGE AND THE BUSINESS CYCLE

Climate change also affects weather, and we can expect to experience more severe and catastrophic droughts, floods, hurricanes, and tornados. These natural disasters will affect global food production, commerce, and economic activity. Recent disasters include Hurricane Sandy (2012), which hit New Jersey and New York at an estimated cost of $65 billion; the great western drought of 2012, which cost an estimated $30 billion; and the "super" tornados in April 2011 that hit Alabama (estimated cost: $10 billion) and Missouri in May 2011 (estimated cost: $9 billion). The periodicity of these events will add to the overall cyclical ebb and flow of the economy. Destruction of property will cause more business activity to rebuild damaged property and replace equipment. Insurance companies will become stressed in handling the increase in activity, and higher premiums will certainly result.[186]

These events are occurring with greater frequency and at a greater cost. The paper "US Billion-Dollar Weather and Climate Disasters," by Smith and Katz shows that events of weather- and climate-related disasters resulting in over $1 billion in damages are increasing at a rate of almost 5% per year. (See Figure 23 for a graph of the trend since 1980.) This information should shock even the most casual observer to the profound truth of the data, which is, climate change is significant and undeniable – and its impact is getting worse.[187]

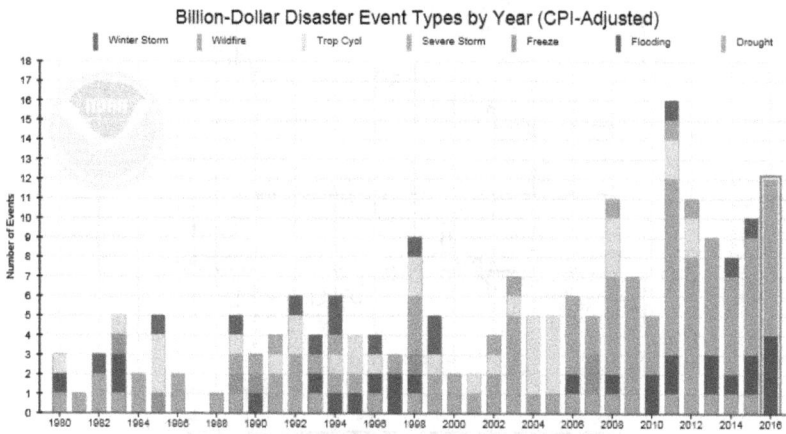

Billion-Dollar Disaster Event Types by Year (CPI-Adjusted)

Figure 23. Weather Disasters Resulting in $1 Billion in Damages or More[188]

The authors of this paper further analyzed this data and they provided some statistical analysis. The data were fitted with a Poisson curve that is statistically significant (meaning, it is not random), and it shows an observable and verified trend in the data. The fact that the curve is exponentially increasing is shocking and should be a major concern for political leadership worldwide.

Not only are weather extremes changing, but weather patterns are changing also. There are more areas of extreme drought and extreme flooding than ever before. In particular, the weather patterns in Africa have changed within the last 50 years, such that areas that used to have constant rainfall no longer have measurable precipitation. Figure 24 shows how there used to be a 50/50 split of rainfall above and below the 35th parallel. Since about the year 1960, that number has been diverging from the even split to favoring the more northern latitudes. Now that split is verging on 70% above the 35th parallel and 30% below the 35th parallel. This could account for the constant drought conditions in northern Africa, and it could explain why lakes such as Lake Chad are virtually disappearing.[189]

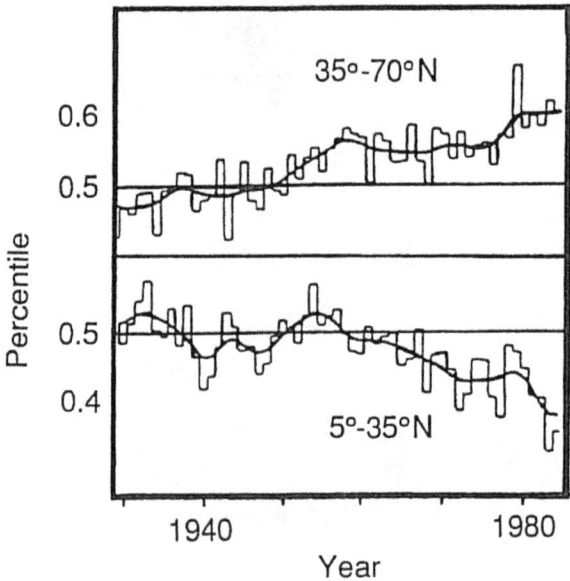

Figure 24. Rainfall in Europe and Northern Africa, 1930–1985

POLITICAL, ECOLOGICAL, AND TECHNOLOGICAL CHANGE

I have described the geopolitical and ecological challenges to the worldwide economy and the US economy in particular. Inflation will certainly be a factor, as well as actions and reactions to political events. A terrorist plot or a nuclear event could also trigger the next crisis. It remains to be seen how Israel responds to a nuclear-capable Iran, or how the civil wars in Syria and Iraq are resolved. We also don't know how far North Korea is from obtaining an operational nuclear weapon – we certainly have all seen and heard the threats coming from Pyongyang. The world continues to be a dangerous place, and political and economic land mines abound. All these factors contribute to what could potentially be a worldwide crisis in the near future.

What will be the next technological innovation that will dominate the economy? Would it be related to nanotechnology, genetics, or energy? I personally believe it will be related to energy, because that will be the single most challenging aspect of our future – our dependence on foreign oil as the lubricant of our economy. As I have said before, I believe that Hubbert's Peak will come to fruition and, try as it might, there will be no way for the country to handle this worldwide economic shock. It will come like a day of reckoning, and we will all suffer the consequences. Unless this country does something soon to affect that outcome, our fate will be sealed, and we will spend the rest of the century sorting it out.

Epilogue

Everything has a cycle. There is a periodicity to everything. The key factor in determining in what direction things are headed is in understanding where you are on that curve. In order for you to know what's next, you need to know where you've been and what road you're on. What's next for the economy will depend on the intersection and influence of the different cycles overlaid on each other.

All these cycles are interrelated: inflation, the stock market, real estate, and the business cycle. What's next could be different, depending on the confluence of the different cycles overlapping. Depending on where you are in each of these curves, you can predict what the general overall future will be in any of these cycles. This is a good thing to know. And based on that location, you can guide your decisions toward a path of profitability and success. It's just like navigation: If you don't know where you are, it's hard to figure out where you should go or where you will end up.

I have written this book to contain the summation of my over 50 years of life experience and over 30 years of work experience, as I interpret it and understand it. I have made plenty of financial mistakes in the past, and hopefully you can learn from my experiences. I have studied the real estate market and stock market extensively, and I have had both positive and negative results. My own personal observations are just that – observations and life lessons from an average guy trying to get ahead. The reason I say I am average is because it seems as if over the past 35+ years, every event that has affected the average American has also affected me.

As an engineer and systems analyst, project manager, and integrated product team leader, I try to look at the big picture and use data and metrics to help me make decisions. What I have seen over the years is that teams and programs and organizations tend to maintain the performance of their past, and it is difficult to expect anything to change. It is with this perspective that I have provided the hypothesis that cycles will repeat themselves, and we can't expect things to change. I hope I have provided enough information, enough data for you to perform your own decision analysis and come to your own conclusions about the veracity of my observations.

In the introduction to the 1997 printing of his classic book *The Great Crash, 1929*, John Kenneth Galbraith stated that it is better not to provide predictions, because people will only remember when you are wrong and they won't give you credit when you are correct. Perhaps I should have heeded his advice and not been so presumptive in my views that history repeats itself – that we should take lessons in these observations of history. However, I stand by my observations and my beliefs, and it is my sincere wish that individuals, households, and businesses would find this information useful in planning and achieving their financial goals.

Good luck to all of you.

Notes

Below are the references I used to create this book. I have tried to err on the side of too much documentation, rather than too little, for two reasons: 1) to show my work and indicate how I came to my conclusions, and 2) to provide readers references for the purposes of their own investigations.

Section I, Chapter 1:

1 *The Great Inflation and Its Aftermath (The Past and Future of American Affluence)* by Robert J. Samuelson, 2008, Random House Publishing Group, New York, New York, page 47

2 *Ibid*, page 58

3 Statement by Ben S. Bernanke, Chairman Board of Governors of the Federal Reserve System, before the Committee on Financial Services, US House of Representatives, July 17, 2013

4 US Bureau of Labor and Statistics website, www.bls.gov

5 *Ibid*

6 *The American President, A Complete History*, by Kathryn Moore, 2007, Fall River Press, New York, New York, page 471

7 *Updated Estimates of the Effects of the Insurance Coverage Provisions of the Affordable Care Act, April 2014*, Congressional Budget Office (CBO), Publication Number 4930

8 www.treasurydirect.gov, Public Debt Reports, Monthly Statement of the Public Debt of the United States, December 31, 2016

9 *Time and Chance: Gerald Ford's Appointment With History*, by James Cannon, 1994, HarperCollins Publishers, Inc., New York, New York, page 402

10 *The Great Inflation and Its Aftermath (The Past and Future of American Affluence)* by Robert J. Samuelson, 2008, Random House Publishing Group, New York, New York, pages 94-96

11 *Time and Chance: Gerald Ford's Appointment With History*, by James Cannon, 1994, HarperCollins Publishers, Inc., New York, New York, page 414

12 *Nixon's Economy – Booms, Busts, Dollars, and Votes*, by Allen J. Matusow, 1998, University Press of Kansas, Lawrence, Kansas, page 158

13 *Ibid*, pages 164-166

14 *The Great Inflation and Its Aftermath (The Past and Future of American Affluence)* by Robert J. Samuelson, 2008, Random House Publishing Group, New York, New York, pages 99-100

15 "Inflation and War" figure used by permission of A. Gary Shilling & Co, Inc

16 US Bureau of Labor and Statistics website, www.bls.gov

17 *The Fed: The Inside Story of How the World's Most Powerful Financial Institution Drives the Markets*, by Martin Mayer, 2001, The Free Press (A Division of Simon & Schuster, Inc.), New York, New York, page 204

18 *The Great Inflation and Its Aftermath (The Past and Future of American Affluence)* by Robert J. Samuelson, 2008, Random House Publishing Group, New York, New York, page 105

19 US Bureau of Labor and Statistics website, www.bls.gov

20 *Ibid*

Section I, Chapter 2:

21   http://www.freeby50.com/2009/04/cost-of-computers-overtime. Html

22 *The Great Depression: An Inquiry into the Causes, Course, and Consequences of the Worldwide Depression of the Nineteen-Thirties, as Seen by Comparison and in the Light of History*, by John A Garrary, 1986, Harcourt Brace Jovanovich Publishers, Orlando Florida, page 245

23 *Ibid*, page 15

24 Excerpts from THE GREAT CRASH 1929 by John Kenneth Galbraith. Copyright © 1954, 1955, 1961, 1972, 1988, 1997 by John Kenneth Galbraith. Reprinted by permission of Houghton Mifflin Harcourt Publishing Company. All rights reserved.

25 http://www.history.com/topics/great-depression

26 http://useconomy.about.com/od/grossdomesticproduct/p/1929_Depression.htm

27 http://www.u-s-history.com/pages/h1569.html

28 http://history1900s.about.com/od/1930s/p/greatdepression.htm

29 www.NBER.org

30 *Supercycles*, by Arun Motianey, 2010, McGraw-Hill Publishing Company, New York, New York, page 26

31 *The Intelligent Investor*, by Benjamin Graham, 1973, Revised Edition with Commentary by Jason Zweig, 2003, HarperCollins Publishers, Inc., New York, New York, page 58

32 *Ibid*, page 62

33 Speech by Ben S. Bernanke, Chairman Board of Governors of the Federal Reserve System, "The First 100 Years of the Federal Reserve: The Policy Record, Lessons Learned, and Prospects for the Future," at a conference sponsored by the National Bureau of Economic Research, Cambridge, Massachusetts, July 10, 2013

34 *The Boom and the Bubble*, by Robert Brenner, 2002, Verso, New York, New York, page 112

35 *Volcker, The Triumph of Persistence*, by William L. Silber, 2012, Bloomsbury Press, New York, New York, page 254

36 *The Boom and the Bubble*, by Robert Brenner, 2002, Verso, New York, New York, page 130

Section I, Chapter 3:

37 *Cycles: The Science of Prediction*, by Edward R. Dewey and Edwin F. Dakin, 1947, Henry Holt and Company, Inc., New York, New York, page 70

38 "Kondratieff Cycle" figure used by permission of A. Gary Shilling & Co, Inc

39 *The Long Wave Cycle*, by Nikolai Kondratieff, as translated by Gary Daniels, 1984, Richardson & Snyder Publishing, pages 64-67, 70, 75, and 79

40 *The New New Deal*, by Michael Grunwald, 2012, Simon & Schuster, Inc., New York, New York, page 4

41 *The Long Wave Cycle*, by Nikolai Kondratieff, as translated by Gary Daniels, 1984, Richardson & Snyder Publishing, page 12

42 *The Fed's Thermostat*, by Milton Friedman, The Wall Street Journal, August 19, 2003

43 Statement by Ben S. Bernanke, Chairman Board of Governors of the Federal Reserve System, before the Committee on Financial Services US House of Representatives, July 17, 2013

44 *The Fed: The Inside Story of How the World's Most Powerful Financial Institution Drives the Markets*, by Martin Mayer, 2001, The Free Press (A Division of Simon & Schuster, Inc.), New York, New York, page 165

45 "More drought predicted: NOAA reports the dry conditions will continue to cause problems in much of the US, especially in the West," by Neela Banerjee, *The Los Angeles Times*, February 22, 2013

46 "The Mississippi is all choked up: Low water flows because of drought jam up barge traffic. Food prices could rise," by Julie Cart, *The Los Angeles Times*, September 2, 2012

47 *The Great Wave: Price Revolutions and the Rhythm of History*, by David Hackett Fischer, 1996, Oxford University Press, Inc., New York, New York, page 233

Section I, Chapter 4:

48 *Cycles: The Science of Prediction*, by Edward R. Dewey and Edwin F. Dakin, 1947, Henry Holt and Company, Inc., New York, New York, pages 96-97

49 *The Great Reflation: How Investors Can Profit from the New World of Money*, by J. Anthony Boeckh, 2010, John Wiley & Sons, Inc., Hoboken, New Jersey, page 84

50 *Out of Gas: The End of the Age of Oil*, by David Goodstein, 2004, W. W. Norton & Company, Inc., New York, New York, page 18

51 *Ibid*, page 30

52 *Winner Take All: China's Race for Resources and What It Means for the World*, by Dambisa Moyo, 2012, Basic Books, New York, New York, page 17

53 *Hubbert's Peak: The Impending World Oil Shortage*, by Kenneth S. Deffeyes, 2001, Princeton University Press, Princeton, New Jersey, page 9

54 "US affirms support for Japan in islands dispute with China," by Mark Feisenthal and David Alexander, www.reuters.com, November 27, 2013

55 "Q&A: South China Sea dispute, Rival countries have wrangled over territory in the South China Sea for centuries – but a recent upsurge in tension has sparked concerns that the area is becoming a flashpoint with global consequences," 15 May 2013, www.bbc.com/news/world-asiapacific-13748349

56 "Trying to excavate a future for Afghans: The country is rich in minerals, but building a mining industry will be a rocky road," by Alexandra Zavis, *The Los Angeles Times*, March 24, 2013

57 "Myanmar struggles to pivot away from China," by Mark Magnier, *The Los Angeles Times*, March 24, 2013

58 *$20 Per Gallon: How the Inevitable Rise in the Price of Gasoline Will Change Our Lives for the Better,* by Christopher Steiner, 2009, Grand Central Publishing, Hachette Book Group, New York, New York page 157

59 "American businesses are nervous about the Chinese New Year," by Parija Kavilanz, January 20, 2011, CNNMoney.com

60 "Truckers trickle back to work in Shanghai after strike over costs," by David Pierson and Lauren Hilgers, *The Los Angeles Times*, April 26, 2011

61 *Winner Take All: China's Race for Resources and What It Means for the World,* by Dambisa Moyo, 2012, Basic Books, New York, New York

62 http://www.cnbc.com/id/45291217, CNBC Transcript: Warren Buffett on China, the Economy, and Corporate Jet Tax Breaks (Part 7), Alex Crippen, Monday, 14 Nov 2011

63 *Hubbert's Peak: The Impending World Oil Shortage,* by Kenneth S. Deffeyes, 2001, Princeton University Press, Princeton, New Jersey, pg 11

64 *Ibid*

65 "Killing in L.A. Drops to 1967 Levels: Despite the faltering economy, homicides decline to one of the lowest rates among major US cities," by Joel Rubin and Robert Faturechi, *The Los Angeles Times*, December 27, 2010 (graphic by *Thomas Suh Lauder*, Copyright © 2010 Los Angeles Times, Reprinted with Permission)

66 *The Great Wave, Price Revolutions and the Rhythm of History,* by David Hackett Fischer, 1996, Oxford University Press, Inc., New York, New York, page 226, by permission of Oxford University Press, USA

Section II, Chapter 5:

67 *The Market's Measure: An Illustrated History of America Told Through the Dow Jones Industrial Average,* Edited by John A. Prestbo, 1999, Dow Jones & Company, Inc., New York, New York, page 105

68 *The Great Boom, 1950-2000: How a Generation of Americans Created the World's Most Prosperous Society,* by Robert Sobel, 2000, Truman Talley Books, St. Martin's Press, New York, New York, page 394

69 *Remembering Netscape: The Birth Of The Web*, by Adam Lashinsky, *Fortune* Magazine, July 25, 2005

70 *Irrational Exuberance*, by Robert J. Shiller, 2005, Princeton University Press, Princeton, New Jersey, page 2

71 *Steve Jobs*, by Walter Isaacson, 2011, Simon & Schuster, New York, New York, pages 325-326

72 *The Great Boom, 1950-2000: How a Generation of Americans Created the World's Most Prosperous Society*, by Robert Sobel, 2000, Truman Talley Books, St. Martin's Press, New York, New York, page 408

73 US Bureau of the Census, Merchant Wholesalers, Except Manufacturers' Sales Branches and Offices Sales: Durable Goods: Professional and Commercial Equipment and Supplies Sales: Computer and Computer Peripheral Equipment and Software Sales [S42343M144SCEN], retrieved from FRED, Federal Reserve Bank of St. Louis; https://fred.stlouisfed.org/series/S42343M144SCEN

74 *The Age of Turbulence: Adventures in a New World*, by Alan Greenspan, 2007, Penguin Books, New York, New York, page 204

75 *Ibid*, page 205

76 "Eighty Years After The Great Crash – 'Is It the 30s Again?'," by Brett Arends and Dave Kansas, *The Wall Street Journal*, reprinted in *The Orange County Register*, Sunday edition, October 18, 2009

77 "Krispy Kreme Franchise Buybacks May Spur New Concerns," by Mark Maremont and Rick Brooks, *The Wall Street Journal*, May 25, 2004

Section II, Chapter 6:

78 Excerpts from THE GREAT CRASH 1929 by John Kenneth Galbraith. Copyright © 1954, 1955, 1961, 1972, 1988, 1997 by John Kenneth Galbraith. Reprinted by permission of Houghton Mifflin Harcourt Publishing Company. All rights reserved.

79 *Business Cycles: A Theoretical, Historical, and Statistical Analysis of the Capitalist Process*, by Joseph A. Schumpeter, 1939, McGraw-Hill, New York, New York, page 909

80 *Ibid*, page 911

81 *Ibid*, pages 950-954

82 Excerpts from THE GENERAL THEORY OF EMPLOYMENT INTEREST AND MONEY copyright © 1965 by John Maynard Keynes. Reprinted by permission of Houghton Mifflin Harcourt Publishing Company. All rights reserved.

83 Excerpts from THE GREAT CRASH 1929 by John Kenneth Galbraith. Copyright © 1954, 1955, 1961, 1972, 1988, 1997 by John Kenneth Galbraith. Reprinted by permission of Houghton Mifflin Harcourt Publishing Company. All rights reserved.

84 Excerpts from THE GREAT CRASH 1929 by John Kenneth Galbraith. Copyright © 1954, 1955, 1961, 1972, 1988, 1997 by John Kenneth Galbraith. Reprinted by permission of Houghton Mifflin Harcourt Publishing Company. All rights reserved.

85 Excerpts from THE GREAT CRASH 1929 by John Kenneth Galbraith. Copyright © 1954, 1955, 1961, 1972, 1988, 1997 by John Kenneth Galbraith. Reprinted by permission of Houghton Mifflin Harcourt Publishing Company. All rights reserved.

86 Excerpts from THE GREAT CRASH 1929 by John Kenneth Galbraith. Copyright © 1954, 1955, 1961, 1972, 1988, 1997 by John Kenneth Galbraith. Reprinted by permission of Houghton Mifflin Harcourt Publishing Company. All rights reserved.

87 *Presidents: All You Need to Know*, by Carter Smith, 2004, Hylas Publishing, Irvington, New York, page 276

Section II, Chapter 7:

88 NYSE EURONEXT, New York Stock Exchange, http://www.nyx.com/who-we-are/history/new-york

89 DOW JONES, Dow Jones History, http://www.dowjones.com/history.asp

90 *History of the Dow: The Dow Jones Averages*, by Randy Befumo and Alex Schay, The Motley Fool, www.fool.com/Ddow/HistoryOfTheDow5.htm

91 *The Panic of 1907: Lessons Learned From the Market's Perfect Storm*, by Robert F. Bruner and Sean D. Carr, 2007, John Wiley & Sons, New York, New York

92 *The New Deal: A Modern History*, by Michael Hilzik, 2011, Free Press, a division of Simon & Schuster, Inc., New York, New York

93 *The Market's Measure: An Illustrated History of America Told Through the Dow Jones Industrial Average*, Edited by John A. Prestbo, 1999, Dow Jones & Company, Inc., New York, New York, page 94

94 *Aftershock: The Next Economy and America's Future*, by Robert B. Reich, 2010, Alfred A. Knopf, a division of Random House, Inc., New York, New York, page 82

95 *The Market's Measure: An Illustrated History of America Told Through the Dow Jones Industrial Average*, Edited by John A. Prestbo, 1999, Dow Jones & Company, Inc., New York, New York, page 111

Section II, Chapter 8:

96 *The Boom and the Bubble*, by Robert Brenner, 2002, Verso, New York, New York, page 194

97 *Irrational Exuberance*, by Robert J. Shiller, 2005, Princeton University Press, Princeton, New Jersey, page 47

98 *The Coming Economic Collapse: How You Can Thrive When Oil Costs $200 a Barrel*, by Stephen Leeb and Glen Strathy, 2006, Warner Business Books, Warner Books, New York, New York, pages 170-180

99 *Rainbow's End: The Crash of 1929*, by Maury Klein, 2001, Oxford University Press, New York, New York, page 93

100 *Irrational Exuberance*, by Robert J. Shiller, 2005, Princeton University Press, Princeton, New Jersey, page 9

101 *Dow 40,000: Strategies for Profiting from the Greatest Bull Market in History*, by David Elias, 1999, McGraw-Hill, New York, New York

Section III, Chapter 9:

102 *Dutch, A Memoir of Ronald Regan*, by Edmund Morris, 1999, Random House, New York, New York, page 446

103 "Take It From Japan: Bubbles Hurt," by Martin Fackler, *The New York Times*, December 25, 2005

104 *Inside Job: The Looting of America's Savings and Loans*, by Stephen Pizzo, Mary Fricker, and Paul Muolo, 1989, McGraw-Hill Publishing Company, New York, New York, pages 269-271

105 *Trust Me: Charles Keating and the Missing Billions*, by Michael Binstein and Charles Bowden, 1993, Random House, Inc., New York, New York, pages 287-290

106 *Inside Job: The Looting of America's Savings and Loans*, by Stephen Pizzo, Mary Fricker, and Paul Muolo, 1989, McGraw-Hill Publishing Company, New York, New York, page 13

107 *Ibid*, page 21

108 *Ibid*, page 20

109 *Ibid*, pages 30-37

110 *Ibid*, page 60

111 *Ibid*, page 228

112 *Ibid*, page 60

Section III, Chapter 10:

113 *After The Music Stopped: The Financial Crisis, the Response, and the Work Ahead*, by Alan S. Blinder, 2013, The Penguin Press, New York, New York, page 66

114 "Duarte Sounds Budget Alarm; City leaders consider declaring a fiscal crisis so they can ask voters to raise the sales tax," by Abby Sewell, *The Los Angeles Times*, July 31, 2012

115 "New city already in crisis; State legislators have raided the frugal Jurupa Valley's money," by Phil Willon, *The Los Angeles Times*, July 30, 2012

116 "Real Estate Gold Rush: Inside the hot-money world of housing speculators, condo flippers, and get-rich-quick schemers. (Is it too late to get in?)," by Grainger David, *Fortune* magazine, May 30, 2005

117 *Real Estate Guide 2005*, *Money* magazine, June 2005

118 *Irrational Exuberance*, by Robert J. Shiller, 2005, Princeton University Press, Princeton, New Jersey, page 44

119 "Take It From Japan, Bubbles Hurt," by Martin Fackler, *The New York Times*, December 25, 2005

120 *Irrational Exuberance*, by Robert J. Shiller, 2005, Princeton University Press, Princeton, New Jersey, page 40

121 *The Trillion Dollar Meltdown: Easy Money, High Rollers, and the Great Credit Crash*, by Charles R. Morris, 2008, PublicAffairs, a member of the Perseus Books Group, New York, New York, page 67

122 *The Subprime Solution: How Today's Global Financial Crisis Happened and What to Do About It*, by Robert J. Shiller, reproduced with permission of author via email and permission of Princeton University Press via Copyright Clearance Center

123 *Irrational Exuberance*, by Robert J. Shiller, 2005, Princeton University Press, Princeton, New Jersey, page xviii

124 *Decision Points*, by George W. Bush, 2010, Crown Publishers, a division of Random House, Inc., New York, New York, page 449

125 *The New New Deal: The Hidden Story of Change in the Obama Era*, by Michael Grunwald, 2012, Simon & Schuster, Inc., New York, New York, page 15

Section III, Chapter 11:

126 *The Great 18-Year Real Estate Cycle*, by Steve H. Hanke, Globe Asia, February 2010

127 *The Depression of 2008*, by Fred E. Foldvary, 2007, The Guttenberg Press, Berkeley, California

128 *Cycles: The Science of Prediction*, by Edward R. Dewey and Edwin F. Dakin, 1947, Henry Holt and Company, Inc., New York, New York, page 124

129 *Ibid*, page 125-126

130 *Ibid*, pages 127

131 *Levittown, Two Families, One Tycoon, and the Fight for Civil Rights in America's Legendary Suburb,* by David Kushner, 2009, Walker Publishing Company, Inc., New York, New York, page 36

132 *Ibid*, page 39

133 *Irrational Exuberance*, by Robert J. Shiller, 2005, Princeton University Press, Princeton, New Jersey, page 13

134 *Spectral Analysis of World GDP Dynamics: Kondratieff Waves, Kuznets Swings, Juglar and Kitchin Cycles in Global Economic Development, and the 2008–2009 Economic Crisis*, by Andrey Koroyatev and Sergey Tsirel, 2010, Structure and Dynamics: eJournal of Anthropological and Related Sciences, Volume 4, Issue 1, UC Irvine, Irvine, California

135 *Ibid*

136 *Cycles: The Science of Prediction*, by Edward R. Dewey and Edwin F. Dakin, 1947, Henry Holt and Company, Inc., New York, New York, page 115

137 *Ibid*, page 123

138 *The Trillion Dollar Meltdown: Easy Money, High Rollers, and the Great Credit Crash*, by Charles R. Morris, 2008, PublicAffairs, a member of the Perseus Books Group, New York, New York, page 66

139 US Census Bureau, New Home Sales, Annual Rate for New Singlefamily Houses Sold: United States, Seasonally Adjusted All Houses [Thousands of Units], 1963-2013

Section III, Chapter 12:

140 Board of Governors of the Federal Reserve System (US), Effective Federal Funds Rate [FEDFUNDS], retrieved from FRED, Federal Reserve Bank of St. Louis; https://fred.stlouisfed.org/series/FEDFUNDS

141 "5 States Where Homeowners Lost the Most Money," by Anna Maria Andriotis, www.MarketWatch.com, November 15, 2013

142 *The Next Hundred Million: America in 2050*, by Joel Kotkin, 2010, Penguin Press, New York, New York

143 US Census Bureau, New Residential Construction, Annual Rate for Housing Units Authorized in Permit-Issuing Places: United States, Seasonally Adjusted Total Units [Thousands of Units], 1960-2013

Section IV, Chapter 13:

144 *The American President: A Complete History*, by Kathryn Moore, 2007, Fall River Press, New York, New York, page 584

145 *My Life*, by Bill Clinton, 2004, Random House, Inc., New York, New York, pages 451-452

146 *The Agenda: Inside the Clinton White House*, by Bob Woodward, 1994, Simon & Schuster, New York, New York, pages 69-71

147 *Ibid*, pages 82-90

148 *My Life*, by Bill Clinton, 2004, Random House, Inc., New York, New York, pages 522 and 533-537

149 *The American President: A Complete History*, by Kathryn Moore, 2007, Fall River Press, New York, New York, page 602

150 *Maestro: Greenspan's Fed and the American Boom*, by Bob Woodward, 2000, Simon & Schuster, New York, New York, page 144

151 *The Age of Turbulence: Adventures in a New World*, by Alan Greenspan, 2007, Penguin Books, New York, New York, page 188

152 *When Genius Failed: The Rise and Fall of Long-Term Capital Management*, by Roger Lowenstein, 2000, Random House Trade Paperback, Random House, Inc., New York, New York, pages 144-147

153 *Maestro: Greenspan's Fed and the American Boom*, by Bob Woodward, 2000, Simon & Schuster, New York, New York, pages 199-206

154 *When Washington Shut Down Wall Street: The Great Financial Crisis of 1914 and the Origins of America's Monetary Supremacy*, by William L. Silber, 2007, Princeton University Press, Princeton, New Jersey, pages 2-3

Section IV, Chapter 14:

155 *Beyond the Crash, Overcoming the First Crisis of Globalization,* by Gordon Brown, 2010, Free Press, a Division of Simon & Schuster, Inc., New York, New York, page 21

156 *Fool's Gold, How the Bold Dream of a Small Tribe at J.P. Morgan Was Corrupted by Wall Street Greed and Unleashed a Catastrophe,* by Gillian Tett, 2009, Free Press, a Division of Simon & Schuster, Inc., New York, New York, pages 220-222

157 *On the Brink: Inside the Race to Stop the Collapse of the Global Financial System*, by Henry M. Paulson, Jr., 2010, Business Plus, Hachette Book Group, New York, New York, pages 137-170

158 *Too Big to Fail: The Inside Story of How Wall Street and Washington Fought to Save the Financial System from Crisis – and Themselves,* by Andrew Ross Sorkin, 2009, Viking Penguin, a member of Penguin Group (USA) Inc., New York, New York, page 352

159 *After The Music Stopped: The Financial Crisis, the Response, and the Work Ahead*, by Alan S. Blinder, 2013, The Penguin Press, New York, New York, page 136

160 *On the Brink: Inside the Race to Stop the Collapse of the Global Financial System*, by Henry M. Paulson, Jr., 2010, Business Plus, Hachette Book Group, New York, New York, pages 250-329

161 *Larry Crowne*, 2011, Universal Pictures, Venome Pictures, Playtone Productions

162 *Winner Take All: China's Race for Resources and What It Means for the World*, by Dambisa F. Moyo, 2012, Basic Books, a member of Perseus Books Group, New York, New York, page 177

Section IV, Chapter 15:

163 *Business Cycles: A Theoretical, Historical, and Statistical Analysis of the Capitalist Process*, by Joseph A. Schumpeter, 1939, McGraw-Hill, New York, New York, page 165

164 *Ibid*, page 173

165 *Ibid*, page 173

166 *Ibid*, page 213

167 *Ibid*, page 130

168 *Ibid*, pages 135-137

169 *Ibid*, pages 150-157

170 *Ibid*, page 86

171 *Cycles: The Science of Prediction*, by Edward R. Dewey and Edwin F. Dakin, 1947, Henry Holt and Company, Inc., New York, New York, pages 75-76

172 *Ibid*, page 84

173 *Ibid*, page 93

174 *Ibid*, page 92

175 *Ibid*, pages 90-91

176 *Ibid*, page 96

177 *Business Cycles: A Theoretical, Historical, and Statistical Analysis of the Capitalist Process*, by Joseph A. Schumpeter, 1939, McGraw-Hill, New York, New York, page 213

178 Excerpts from THE GENERAL THEORY OF EMPLOYMENT INTEREST AND MONEY copyright © 1965 by John Maynard Keynes. Reprinted by permission of Houghton Mifflin Harcourt Publishing Company. All rights reserved.

179 Excerpts from THE GENERAL THEORY OF EMPLOYMENT INTEREST AND MONEY copyright © 1965 by John Maynard Keynes. Reprinted by permission of Houghton Mifflin Harcourt Publishing Company. All rights reserved.

180 Excerpts from THE GENERAL THEORY OF EMPLOYMENT INTEREST AND MONEY copyright © 1965 by John Maynard Keynes. Reprinted by permission of Houghton Mifflin Harcourt Publishing Company. All rights reserved.

181 *The Well-Timed Strategy: Managing the Business Cycle for Competitive Advantage*, by Peter Navarro, 2006, Pearson Education, Inc., publishing as Wharton School Publishing, Upper Saddle River, New Jersey, pages 190-192

182 *Ibid*, pages 192-197

Section IV, Chapter 16:

183 Federal Reserve Press Release, *Release Date: December 18, 2013*

184 *Ibid*

185 "Greenland's Snow Hides 100 Billion Tons of Water," by Becky Oskin, www.Yahoo.com, 12/23/13

186 www.Planetsave.com and www.NOAA.gov

187 "US Billion-Dollar Weather and Climate Disasters: Data Sources, Trends, Accuracy, and Biases," by Adam B. Smith and Richard W. Katz, this article has been accepted for publication in the journal Natural Hazards, the pre-publication version is available at http://link.springer.com/article/10.1007/s11069-013-0566-5

188 NOAA National Centers for Environmental Information (NCEI) U.S. Billion-Dollar Weather and Climate Disasters (2016). https://www.ncdc.noaa.gov/billions/

About the Author

Edward Thomas is a member of the Royal Economic Society. He received a Master of Business Administration from the University of California in Irvine, California and was a National Merit Scholar at the University of Michigan in Ann Arbor, Michigan.

Edward Thomas has worked in the Aerospace industry as a project manager and product leader on missile programs (Minuteman and Peacekeeper), airplane programs (Stealth Bomber, Boeing 787, and Boeing P-8A), and space programs (International Space Station and X-37). He used quantitative data and predictive metrics to determine how well things were going, and what to expect in the future (from a schedule and cost performance perspective). He has applied that experience and other life lessons to the business of economics and personal finance, and the result is this book. You can follow him on Twitter @MoneyWeatherMan or read his blog at www.EdwardThomasAuthor.com to get his latest insights on what is happening in the markets, or to find where we are in the business cycle, and how changes in the economy will affect your finances.

Acknowledgments

I would like to thank my family and friends for their love and support. I would also like to thank the following people and organizations for their help in bringing this book to fruition: Judith Briles and the folks at AuthorU for their insights and information about the publishing industry, Dr. Terry Burnham for his time discussing economics and publishing, Gabriella Deponte for her editing work and interesting stories about investment banking, Dr. David Hackett Fischer, Timothy Bent (OUP), and Mary Bergin-Cartwright (OUP) for permissions from *The Great Wave*, Dr. Fred Foldvary for permissions from *The Depression of 2008*, Mary Fricker for sharing her knowledge of repurchase borrowing (shadow banking) and blogs, Ronald Hussey for permissions from Houghton Mifflin Harcourt, Meghan Kilduff for clarifying permissions on *Cycles: The Science Of Prediction*, Tai Lopez for providing information and inspiration to book readers everywhere, Maurizio Martino for clarifying copyrights on *Business Cycles*, Dr. Peter Navarro for teaching me about "The Power of Macroeconomics," the Orange County Public Library (OCPL) for their services and staff support, Stephen Pizzo for permission to use excerpts from *Inside Job, The Looting of America's Savings and Loans*, the late Jim Rohn for his philosophical teachings and books about success and life, Fred Rossi for permissions from A. Gary Shilling & Co., Dr. Robert Shiller for his permission to use material from *Irrational Exuberance* and *The Subprime Solution*, Erica Varela for permissions from the *Los Angeles Times*, and Alan Zeleznikar for his review of my manuscript and his thoughts on self-publishing.

Bibliography

Binstein, M. (1993). *Trust Me: Charles Keating and the Missing Billions.* New York, New York: Random House, Inc.

Blinder, A. S. (2013). *After The Music Stopped: The Financial Crisis, the Response, and the Work Ahead.* New York, New York: The Penguin Press.

Boeckh, J. A. (2010). *The Great Reflation: How Investors Can Profit from the New World of Money.* Hoboken, New Jersey: John Wiley & Sons, Inc.

Brenner, R. (2002). *The Boom and the Bubble.* New York, New York: Verso.

Brown, G. (2010). *Beyond the Crash, Overcoming the First Crisis of Globalization.* New York, New York: Free Press, a Division of Simon & Schuster, Inc.

Bruner, R. F. (2007). *The Panic of 1907: Lessons Learned From the Market's Perfect Storm.* New York, New York: John Wiley & Sons.

Bush, G. W. (2010). *Decision Points.* New York, New York: Crown Publishers, a division of Random House, Inc.

Cannon, J. (1994). *Time and Chance: Gerald Ford's Appointment With History.* New York, New York: HarperCollins Publishers, Inc.

Clinton, B. (2004). *My Life.* New York, New York: Random House, Inc.

Deffeyes, K. S. (2001). *Hubbert's Peak: The Impending World Oil Shortage.* Princeton, New Jersey: Princeton University Press.

Dewey, E. R. (1947). *Cycles: The Science of Prediction.* New York, New York: Henry Holt and Company, Inc.

Elias, D. (1999). *Dow 40,000: Strategies for Profiting from the Greatest Bull Market in History.* New York, New York: McGraw-Hill.

Fischer, D. H. (1996). *The Great Wave: Price Revolutions and the Rhythm of History*. New York, New York: Oxford University Press, Inc.

Foldvary, F. E. (2007). *The Depression of 2008*. Berkeley, California: The Guttenberg Press.

Garrary, J. A. (1986). *The Great Depression: An Inquiry into the Causes, Course, and Consequences of the Worldwide Depression of the Nineteen-Thirties, as Seen by Comparison and in the Light of History*. Orlando, Florida: Harcourt Brace Jovanovich Publishers.

Goodstein, D. (2004). *Out of Gas: The End of the Age of Oil*. New York, New York: W. W. Norton & Company, Inc.

Gore, A. (1992). *Earth in the Balance*. New York, New York: Houghton Mifflin Company.

Graham, B. (1973). *The Intelligent Investor*. New York, New York: HarperCollins Publishers, Inc.

Greenspan, A. (2007). *The Age of Turbulence: Adventures in a New World*. New York, New York: Penguin Books.

Grunwald, M. (2012). *The New New Deal: The Hidden Story of Change in the Obama Era*. New York, New York: Simon & Schuster, Inc.

Hilzik, M. (2011). *The New Deal: A Modern History*. New York, New York: Free Press, a division of Simon & Schuster, Inc.

Isaacson, W. (2011). *Steve Jobs*. New York, New York: Simon & Schuster.

Kenneth, G. J. (1954, 1955, 1961, 1972, 1988, 1997). *The Great Crash 1929*. New York, New York: Houghton Mifflin Harcourt Publishing Company.

Keynes, J. M. (1965). *The General Theory of Employment, Interest and Money*. New York, New York: Houghton Mifflin Harcourt Publishing Company.

Klein, M. (2001). *Rainbow's End: The Crash of 1929*. New York, New York: Oxford University Press.

Kondratieff, N. (1984). *The Long Wave Cycle, as translated by Gary Daniels*. New York, New York: Richardson & Snyder Publishing.

Kotkin, J. (2010). *The Next Hundred Million: America in 2050*. New York, New York: Penguin Press.

Kushner, D. (2009). *Levittown, Two Families, One Tycoon, and the Fight for Civil Rights in America's Legendary Suburb.* New York, New York: Walker Publishing Company, Inc.

Leeb, S. (2006). *The Coming Economic Collapse: How You Can Thrive When Oil Costs $200 a Barrel.* New York, New York: Warner Business Books, Warner Books.

Lowenstein, R. (2000). *When Genius Failed: The Rise and Fall of Long-Term Capital Management.* New York, New York: Random House Trade Paperback, Random House, Inc.

Matusow, A. J. (1998). *Nixon's Economy – Booms, Busts, Dollars, and Votes.* Lawrence, Kansas: University Press of Kansas.

Mayer, M. (2001). *The Fed: The Inside Story of How the World's Most Powerful Financial Institution Drives the Markets.* New York, New York: The Free Press (A Division of Simon & Schuster, Inc.).

Moore, K. (2007). *The American President, A Complete History.* New York, New York: Fall River Press.

Morris, C. R. (2008). *The Trillion Dollar Meltdown: Easy Money, High Rollers, and the Great Credit Crash.* New York, New York: PublicAffairs, a member of the Perseus Books Group.

Morris, E. (1999). *Dutch, A Memoir of Ronald Regan.* New York, New York: Random House.

Motianey, A. (2010). *Supercycles.* New York, New York: McGraw-Hill Publishing Company.

Moyo, D. (2012). *Winner Take All: China's Race for Resources and What it Means for the World.* New York, New York: Basic Books.

Paulson, J. H. (2010). *On the Brink: Inside the Race to Stop the Collapse of the Global Financial System.* New York, New York: Business Plus, Hachette Book Group.

Pizzo, S. F. (1989). *Inside Job: The Looting of America's Savings and Loans.* New York, New York: McGraw-Hill Publishing Company.

Prestbo, J. A. (1999). *The Market's Measure: An Illustrated History of America Told Through the Dow Jones Industrial Average.* New York, New York: Dow Jones & Company, Inc.

Reich, R. B. (2010). *Aftershock: The Next Economy and America's Future.* New York, New York: Alfred A. Knopf, a division of Random House, Inc.

Samuelson, R. J. (2008). *The Great Inflation and Its Aftermath (The Past and Future of American Affluence).* New York, New York: Random House Publishing Group.

Schumpeter, J. A. (1939). *Business Cycles: A Theoretical, Historical, and Statistical Analysis of the Capitalist Process.* New York, New York: McGraw-Hill Publishing Company.

Shiller, R. J. (2005). *Irrational Exuberance.* Princeton, New Jersey: Princeton University Press.

Shiller, R. J. (2008). *The Subprime Solution: How Today's Global Financial Crisis Happened and What to Do About It.* Princeton, New Jersey: Princeton University Press.

Silber, W. L. (2007). *When Washington Shut Down Wall Street: The Great Financial Crisis of 1914 and the Origins of America's Monetary Supremacy.* Princeton, New Jersey: Princeton University Press.

Silber, W. L. (2012). *Volcker, The Triumph of Persistence.* New York, New York: Bloomsbury Press.

Smith, C. (2004). *Presidents: All You Need to Know.* Irvington, New York: Hylas Publishing.

Sobel, R. (2000). *The Great Boom, 1950-2000: How a Generation of Americans Created the World's Most Prosperous Society.* New York, New York: Truman Talley Books, St. Martin's Press.

Sorkin, A. R. (2009). *Too Big to Fail: The Inside Story of How Wall Street and Washington Fought to Save the Financial System from Crisis – and Themselves.* New York, New York: Viking Penguin, a member of Penguin Group (USA) Inc.

Steiner, C. (2009). *$20 Per Gallon: How the Inevitable Rise in the Price of Gasoline Will Change Our Lives for the Better,* New York, New York: Grand Central Publishing, Hachette Book Group.

Tett, G. (2009). *Fool's Gold, How the Bold Dream of a Small Tribe at J.P. Morgan Was Corrupted by Wall Street Greed and Unleashed a*

Catastrophe. New York, New York: Free Press, a Division of Simon & Schuster, Inc.

Woodward, B. (1994). *The Agenda: Inside the Clinton White House.* New York, New York: Simon & Schuster.

Woodward, B. (2000). *Maestro: Greenspan's Fed and the American Boom.* New York, New York: Simon & Schuster.

Index